INGRID & REINER KLIMKE

CAVALLETTI
Schooling of horse and rider over ground rails

INGRID & REINER KLIMKE

CAVALLETTI

Schooling of horse and
rider over ground rails

THE LYONS PRESS

Contents

Introduction

The present day interpretation of jumping goes back to the Italian Captain Caprilli. Caprilli's precept of the natural method of schooling at the beginning of last century, led to a complete change of jumping style. Earlier it had been usual for a rider to lean back over an obstacle and to force the horse's neck to be stiff. Caprilli recognised that horses are best able to balance themselves over obstacles, when, by bringing the upper part of his body and his hands forward, the rider takes the weight off his horse's back. Today the *forward* seat is accepted as a matter of course, and one is fully aware that all horses use their necks to balance themselves when they are jumping.

The programme of training by *natural methods* also includes work on the cavalletti. These are wooden rails or poles standing firm on low stands. Caprilli encouraged his horses, with and without the rider, to go over these rails at different gaits. Thus cavalletti work was evolved, and gradually became a clear concept in all Italian Cavalry schools.

In Germany, the training methods of the Italian Jumping School were accepted very slowly. At the Cavalry School at Hanover, Col. von Flotow was generally responsible for the inception of cavalletti work and for the acceptance of basic rules into the formula of the German Equestrian Society. These few rules are still all that we have to go by today.

Books by experts, with the exception of a few general remarks, still only indicate that cavalletti work is a valuable expedient in the schooling of horse and rider.

Practical experience shows us that this is not enough.

One can see riders everywhere who let their horses walk over rails and poles and are thereby quite satisfied that their schooling methods are good. Closer enquiry shows that even the most rudimentary knowledge of the correct distances of the rails for the different gaits is totally absent. The hoped-for success can never possibly be theirs.

Unfortunately, in these cases, the horses are always blamed. Often a good horse has been spoilt through ignorant cavalletti work and has at the same time received serious leg injuries. Some people who have seen this, refuse to consider working a horse over ground poles. It seems necessary, therefore, that a clear-cut description of this type of schooling should be given, not only to warn against injuries or damage but to show the potential benefits that can be obtained through a systematic training over cavalletti.

During my own riding career, I have become convinced by this method of schooling. I was fortunate to see the uses to which cavalletti may be put at the Westphalia Riding and Driving School in Münster, and by different DOK riding instructors in Warendorf. It appealed to me to make full use of my observations and by practise to improve upon them. The many notes made during the following years and the results shown by the horses which I rode in dressage and Olympic trials at shows at home and abroad, encouraged me to try to put my ideas on cavalletti work into a compact treatise.

I should be very happy if readers are thus encouraged and can use these notes to further their own training and that of their horses. I would be particularly happy, if, in the future, there were fewer people, riding their horses over cavalletti without possessing the necessary knowledge as to their use.

Translator's Note

Dr Reiner Klimke needs no introduction to anyone who follows the activities of the gold medallists in dressage. His book does, however, open a new vista in the training of horse and rider in the three disciplines: dressage, showjumping and cross-country, in this country. The theme throughout the book is *never to overtire the horse and to make sure that he enjoys his work*. This is only possible when the horse is ridden by a confident, competent rider who also enjoys a happy relationship with his horse. A rider – be he child or adult – will be confident and competent only when he has taken the trouble to study his horse, to accept good instruction through an instructor and through good books. These three things go hand-in-hand. Obedience from a horse is never obtained by roughness but by understanding, firmness of purpose and systematic schooling. There are no short cuts to success; this comes through a long, painstaking schooling in co-operation between horse and rider. Then the road to success is there for every rider to take if he wishes.

Foreword to the first English edition

I have been much interested in reading this book by Dr Klimke.

The importance of exercises over cavalletti in the training of riding horses for all purposes cannot be over emphasised.

The fact that this book is written by a man who is not only a great expert in the training of the horse, but also one of the greatest exponents of displaying the art, means that it must be of great interest and value to all riders who train their own horses, and I am sure it will be a success.

Brenda Williams

Foreword

It was the wish of many readers to see my book about cavalletti work re-issued. It is over 30 years now since the first issue appeared. Then, as now, the book has been criticised, discussed and written about. The scepticism of many horse people who regarded the work over cavalletti as an unnecessary addition to the training of horses has luckily diminished.

The opposite is in fact true. It has been proved that the work with cavalletti helps progress, especially in the gymnastic work for jumpers.

I am pleased that my daughter Ingrid has agreed to share her experiences as a trainer of national and international showjumpers and put pen to paper. This means that there is a completely new section regarding gymnastic jumping. This was necessary as the development in this area is based on the thoughts of the German Cavalry School which makes use of the information given to us by the breeders of sport horses.

Ingrid has been able to accumulate valuable experiences in all three disciplines – dressage, eventing and showjumping – in which she took part at the highest level and which will enrich this book. It gives the new edition a special value.

It is my wish that the work with cavalletti will find new followers and will add to their pleasure of working with horses and benefit the horses' well-being and bring them success.

Reiner Klimke

Theoretical
Groundwork

Theoretical Groundwork

Let me say right from the start that I have no time for long debates on theory. I always find it difficult to discuss training methods with anyone who apparently knows everything, but who has unfortunately never sat on a horse. On the other hand, I never feel particularly drawn to those horsemen who boast that they have never thoroughly studied riding instruction. Of course, there are riders – especially in jumping – who, thanks to their natural talent, have achieved great success without basic instruction and training. But who can dispute the fact that this talent might have been greatly increased by systematic training?

In other words, I consider theoretical instruction to be an exceptionally valuable complement to practical instruction. Quite a lot of difficulties experienced in training are much more easily overcome if one does not have to rely entirely on one's own perceptivity regarding one's horse, but is forced to stop and think before taking a line of action.

Only a healthy horse, whose condition and muscles have been carefully built up, can produce long-lasting efficient work. The great riders have always considered their horses as partners and not sports implements with which to satisfy their vanity. A partnership cannot exist without responsibility. It is the difference between just sitting on a horse and elevating riding to an art. Those who really love their horses and want to be called riders have the responsibility 'to practise self-discipline and have respect for all living creatures', so said Freiherr von Langen who, after the First World War, made international competition for Germans acceptable again, not only through his exceptional riding but also through his gentlemanly behaviour. (He won a gold medal for dressage in 1928 on the legendary Draufganger.)

The rider is responsible for the health and fitness of his horse. Young people all too often forget this. And unfortunately there are plenty of adult riders who too often think only of their own vanity when they are discussing horses. Often, at horse shows, one can see horses who have been forcibly over-worked for so long that they have completely lost their nerve. People who ride in this way see horses as stupid animals whom they can force to achieve certain results, generally with the use of the stick. It is these people whom we have to blame for the fact that the art of horsemanship is no longer so respected.

The person who really loves his horse and calls himself a horseman is duty bound to practise self-discipline and to respect animals. This responsibility obviously includes the necessity that every rider must first acquire knowledge before he commences the training for which he intends to use certain aids.

When we talk about work with cavalletti, the question of the whys and wherefores immediately arises. Why is it worthwhile to use cavalletti to help train horse and rider? What sort of success can be gained through this method of training? Only when this is quite clear, is there any sense in the following question: How can one make the best use of these opportunities?

What is gained by using cavalletti for training a horse?

The education of a riding horse is the final phase in a series of natural exercises. The horse has to be made fit and his muscles made flexible. The basic strength of the horse should be increased and the joints made more free-moving. Quite a high proportion of his training comes within the sphere of *exercising the muscles* and, in this, cavalletti work is a valuable aid. The development of the muscles is dependent upon stimulation by regular planned exercises. They disappear if they are not used.

This is why cavalletti work is so exceptionally well suited to the development of the muscles, because it requires the horse to undergo *disciplined exercise*. The horse is required to lift his feet higher than normal and therefore to put them down again on the ground more firmly and securely. All four legs and the related muscles are increasingly exercised, without the hoof beats in the three basic gaits being affected. The result is that through the use of engagement and release of the different groups of muscles the horse's movements will be strengthened.

If, however, cavalletti work is overdone, or if the placing of each single rail is not suited to the horse's natural rhythm and action, then there is the danger of serious injury. Muscles improve through exercise only when they are used appropriately to their position and their internal condition. They atrophy if they are compelled to undergo exercise in a false, cramped position, in which they cannot operate properly. The results are swelling and debility caused by metabolic disturbances in the muscles. The reconstruction of new muscle tissue cannot keep pace with the physiological obstruction, so the muscles deteriorate. Only the systematic and slowly increased work over cavalletti can therefore accelerate the build-up of the horse's muscles.

Cavalletti work can also be adapted to *loosen up the muscles* and to ease off *stiffness*, especially with over-worked horses. Horses who are ridden over cavalletti with the neck in a lowered position, are able, for example, to arch their backs and thus relax the back muscles. The horse's movements return to their natural rhythm. After a short time it is possible to see that the action from the hindquarters will be carried over to the forehand without hesitation; the horse's back oscillates and allows the rider to sit comfortably again. Of course, rigid back muscles may be much improved anyway by riding on a loose rein and *lowering the neck* but the correction is easier and simpler if cavalletti are used because then the horse has his movements exactly regulated.

Thus work over cavalletti has the advantage of loosening up and strengthening the horse's muscles. Obviously, it is also useful for the development of the heart and the circulatory system. It is not possible to train separate parts of the body, only the whole body. The gradual but constant increase of exercise improves the efficiency of the circulatory and pulmonary systems and leads to the acquisition of stamina and condition. If cavalletti are used, the rate of improvement of these systems will show a measurable increase.

If one makes use of cavalletti in this programme, then one has the advantage of being able to assess what is required.

One of the first difficulties that a young horse has to overcome, is to learn to balance the weight of his rider. When this problem has been overcome in the riding school, one can begin with *preparations for cross-country riding and jumping*. To arrive at this stage, once more the cavalletti are used. Horses who have been ridden over ground rails acquire a special sure-footedness because their steps, stride and jump have to be adjusted to the immobile ground rails. Apart from this they learn very quickly to adjust their centre of balance. And as their balance is constantly being moved by being made to step higher, the *control of balance* has to be practised and the horse is thus prepared to go safely over uneven ground.

The action of raising the legs at certain distances requires attention and ability to estimate exactly. Thus attributes are called into action which are especially required of showjumpers. So we see that work over cavalletti also gives the rider the chance to get to know his horse and to work on his *psyche*. The manner and the style in which the horse masters his exercises over the cavalletti – whether he is quiet and willing, or puts up a resistance – give clues to his temperament and character. Through using different methods of construction and by varying distances (in a considered and responsible way), the ability to learn can be tested and so encouraged. Horses become quick-witted and, above all, they learn to carry out certain exercises quite independently. Therefore, to a certain extent, cavalletti work is an exercise for the intelligence – a province (alas!) which is far too little understood or valued.

Within the field of *dressage training* cavalletti are especially beneficial to the basic gaits of the walk and trot. Fixed distances between the single rails serve to improve the time and balance of the movement (action). Simply by having to step higher, both carriage and animation are increased. And from there, it is not very far to the first steps of the passage.

The basic question regarding the value of cavalletti work in the riding horse's education, may be answered as follows:

Work over cavalletti makes the basic training of all riding horses easier. They also give the opportunity of overcoming more quickly and easily difficulties in the special arts of jumping, dressage and cross-country.

What is gained by using cavalletti for training the rider

The advantage of cavalletti work for training the rider is equally important. Every sporting occupation exists solely for the pleasure it imparts. Those who ride have got to have enthusiasm and they have got to be willing to accept a certain amount of trouble as well. It is obvious that this enthusiasm requires constant encouragement. This is where riding masters and teachers come in – those who teach in riding schools and clubs, Pony Clubs and the huge number of people who ride simply for pleasure or health. Those teachers who instruct school movements in isolated sections only and have no idea how to make a riding lesson exciting, have only themselves to blame if enthusiasm wears off after a time.

The use of cavalletti, with the many different methods of construction, offers a most welcome change. I have often seen how children, especially, enjoy themselves when one organizes exercises over cavalletti. Generally they enjoy it so much that all shyness and unnaturalness disappears; in a very short time one can see the riders relaxed and supple, going *with* their horses.

So we have come to the practical value of cavalletti in the education of the rider. All beginners find it difficult at the start not to upset their horses by their own position. If the horse gets out of balance almost all beginners try to lean back with the upper part of their bodies and thus harden their hands. This is just the opposite to what is really correct. The hands must *give* so that the horse can use his neck to balance himself. A sudden collapse of the rider onto the back of the saddle upsets the horse's back, instead of helping him. For this reason it is essential for the rider to learn

The uncontrolled movement of the anxious 4-year-old is helped by the balanced seat of the rider.

to *go forward* with the horse. The prerequisite for this is the ability to be able to retain one's balance with a strong knee and thigh grip, independently of the horse's movement. *Knee grip* and *balance control* cannot be practised enough at the beginning. As the action of the horse over cavalletti when cantering is not as high as when showjumping, the work over cavalletti is specially recommended.

Work over the cavalletti provides a lot of fun. It strengthens the seat and educates the feeling of horsemastership. Because of this, it is a necessary complement in the training of *all* riders.

Practical
Equipment

Practical Equipment

Since it is now basically clear what the value of work over cavalletti can mean, we have to go into the question of what equipment is required.

Ground rails of different designs

What do cavalletti look like? In the introduction we observed that ground rails or poles are made of wood, and that the ends are placed firmly on low stands. The poles must be thick, round and hard, so that the horse will pay attention to them, and so that they will not splinter when knocked and cause unnecessary injuries. The most favourable length as a rule is 8–11 ft (2.5–3.5 m). The longer the rails, the more difficult it is to keep the horse going straight.

The supports of the pole can be either square or crossed.

The square stands are usually heavier and make no allowance for increasing the height. Conversely, the crossed stands have the advantage that they can be set at three different heights. For this reason I use only these. The lowest height, which may be regarded as the usual measurement, is about 6–8 in (15–20 cm). It is used especially for work at the walk and trot. At the canter I recommend putting the rails up to 20 in (50 cm) so that the canter movement is properly positive and the horses are taught to pay attention right from the start.

Different types of ground rails.

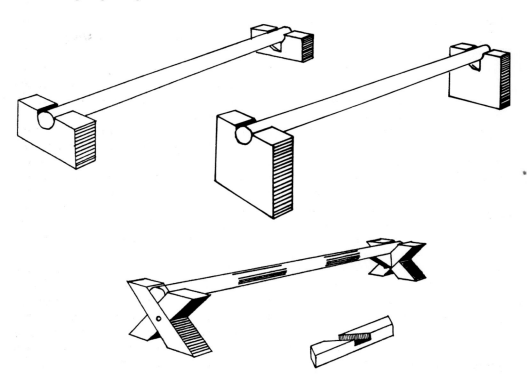

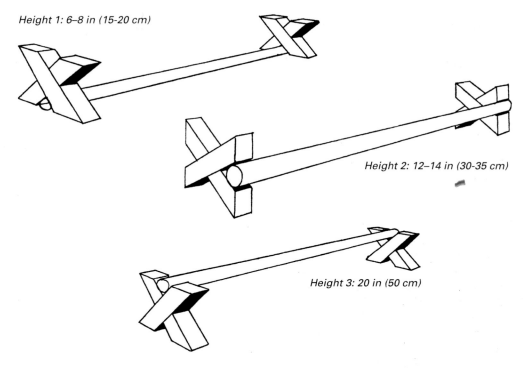

Height 1: 6–8 in (15-20 cm)

Height 2: 12–14 in (30-35 cm)

Height 3: 20 in (50 cm)

Ground rails at three different heights.

Substitute cavalletti: poles

If you have not got the proper cavalletti, you can, with certain restrictions, use substitutes. Poles or rails have disadvantages and therefore, strictly speaking, they are not good substitutes. They cannot be put at the right height of 6–8 in (15–20 cm), thus the horse does not always pay attention to them. Also they move very easily if touched, and they can be dangerous if the horse treads on them as they roll away underfoot. A strained fetlock joint or a pulled tendon could be the result. The cavalletti must be reasonably heavy as light ones move about too easily. Aluminium poles are not suitable; if they are hit, they make a loud noise and can frighten the young horse and discourage the older horse.

Generally speaking four to six rails or poles are sufficient. With the young horse it is a good idea to have some sort of wings at the side.

Condition of the ground

The condition of the ground is of extreme importance and it is far too often overlooked. The amount of work expected of the horse is not entirely governed by the number of cavalletti nor by the time taken in the exercise; it is dependent to a *very great extent* on the state of the ground. Deep or soft going increases the work but has the advantage that there is no jarring of the legs. Hard going does not give and there is the danger of a foot buckling over especially if the stride is uneven.

These consequences must be taken into consideration if cavalletti work is to be successful. If the going is too heavy it puts too much strain on the horse's tendons and ligaments. An option is sand that is not too deep. Care must always be taken that the cavalletti

Cavalletti with sides:
with wings (top);
with poles (bottom).

stands are on even ground where there are no holes.

Tack for the horse

To protect the horse's legs, I always use either boots or bandages. Some people consider this to be overcautious, especially with cross-country horses whose legs have to be hard and used to knocks. Just the same, I prefer to take precautions and protect the legs against hard knocks or brushing injuries. On the other hand, I only use overreach boots in exceptional cases, when horses have shown an inclination to overreach.

I use the normal bridle and saddle for work over cavalletti. Side-reins are not to be used because the horse must be able to stretch his neck forward and downwards as he goes over the obstacle. The following chapter deals with additional exceptions for work without the rider.

Cavalletti work
without the Rider

Cavalletti work without the Rider

Now we can really begin work. We have seen from the earlier chapters that it is necessary to treat the training of the horse and the rider separately. On the one hand we are concentrating solely on the horse and on the other we pay special attention to the balance and firmness of the rider's seat and to the improvement of the rider's ability. In both cases however, each partner learns to know the other, so that both are taught together.

It is *easier* for the horse if he goes over the cavalletti without his rider. He is entirely free and natural since there is no weight to hinder his movements, no hand to pull him backwards and no spur to give him the wrong aid at the wrong moment. So why should we not help him and train him at the start without his rider?

If you take *time* over the basic training and devote the greatest care to the easier exercises, you will later go further much more quickly.

Many young riders cannot see the point of this. If they are ambitious they want success overnight, they cannot be bothered with basic training. Perhaps though, they might be persuaded by the fact that, from the ground, the rider can *see quite a lot* that can be of great value to him. From the saddle, for instance, he cannot see the expression on his horse's face, nor the position of the tail, nor the way the muscles are being used nor the horse's action in all three gaits.

Free movement

If one has the chance to let the horse go free in the school over ground rails, and *not on the lunge*, then this is much to be preferred. It will be seen how much fun this can be and how much the horse *enjoys* his task, as soon as he has understood what is required of him.

It is also important for the horse, before working over cavalletti, to be either led or walked for 10 minutes to supple the joints and to avoid damaging them.

Phase 1: Relaxing on a free rein

Arrange four markers – as in the illustration on page 26 – then allow the horse freedom to canter around without side-reins but with saddle and bridle. This allows him not only to work off surplus energy from standing in the stable but also helps him to loosen up and get the stiffness out of his joints. To let the horse run about uncontrolled, especially if he stops abruptly in the corners, is damaging and should be avoided. It is best to have two helpers in the school to ensure that the horse goes round quietly. Nervous horses should first trot on the lunge and then trot free. It is wrong to turn a horse loose straight out of a stable. The cavalletti are, of course, placed in an enclosed arena or school, and not in the wide open spaces of a paddock where the horse might get away or get into difficulties. Generally 5–10 minutes is enough to let off steam and the horse can then be controlled by the voice and caught.

Phase 2: Adjusting the side-reins

Now comes the second phase whereby the horse has the side-reins attached. Side-reins must be so adjusted as to allow the horse to extend his neck forwards and downwards and thus to arch his back. Therefore they must not be either too short or too long because he must be able to take a contact on them. The proper length is shown in the top photograph (right).

Of course the reins must be the same length on either side, because – contrary to long-reining or lungeing – the horse is now required to go in a straight line.

Now with the side-reins attached, the horse is again allowed to go free and if possible at the trot and canter. After a short time, you will see how the horse, of his own accord, depends upon the kicking boards of the school and, with the help of his trainer and the four markers in the school, keeps to his stride. After about five minutes some horses will go freely along the side of the school. Others require more time and for some, the help of an assistant is needed, see the illustration on page 26. The quieter the trainer and his assistant are, the quicker the horse will settle down.

This is the opportunity to study the horse's *character* and intelligence, and to see if he is willing and quick to understand or if he shows an obstinate contrariness. But it is also a test for the trainer and rider who must remember that in all the arts of equestrianism, both *time* and *patience* are absolutely essential and are the basis of all success.

I have noticed that every horse uses the kicking boards (sides of the school) after a fairly short time. As soon as this has been achieved, the second phase of preparation is finished, and one can begin by building up the ground rails.

Correctly adjusted side-reins.

Attachment of running reins for lungeing.

Phase 3: Trotting over cavalletti

For young horses, it is advisable to erect only one cavalletto at first and slowly increase it to four. Very often with two cavalletti, horses are inclined to think that they have got a spread obstacle in front of them and so they will try to take both rails in one jump. So it is a good idea to place the rails at double the distance apart. Three and four cavalletti are best for trotting work, so this arrangement will come fairly soon. Experienced horses can be schooled almost at once over four cavalletti. The lowest height is chosen: 6–8 in (15–20 cm). I do not recommend more than four cavalletti as I have proved that horses generally become excitable and feel that too much is being asked of them.

The *trot* is the best gait for schooling purposes. At the walk the side-reins often prevent impulsion from the hindquarters. Apart from this, it is much more difficult to keep the horse up to a lively rhythm/cadence at the walk on the track. And without side-reins the whole operation will be valueless because the back muscles are not going to be used. At the beginning, cantering over cavalletti should be avoided because it takes up too much energy.

The *distance* between each ground rail for trot is 4 ft 2 in–5ft (1.3–1.5 m). At the start the right distance will generally speaking be 4 ft 3 in (1.3 m). But it is the rider's job, little by little, to find the correct distance that suits his horse. The height of the rails remains at 6–8 in (15–20 cm) so that the muscles are not overstrained.

When this exercise has been completed, the horse is allowed to trot on whichever rein he prefers. Generally it will be the left rein. It is too much to expect that the horse will trot of his own accord over the rails. Often he will become excitable and will try to gallop over the cavalletti as fast as possible. It looks rather dangerous but, in fact, it really is not. You should leave the horse alone and wait for him to take up the trot again. The only thing you can do at this stage, is to talk to him quietly.

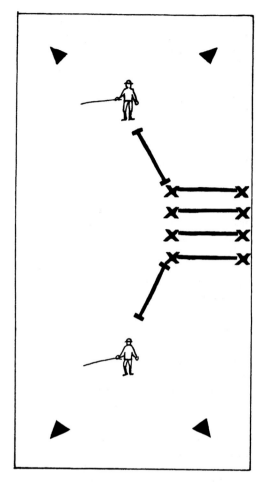

Layout of cavalletti for loose jumping in a school.

He will not be able to run out because of the markers and the wings. If a horse stops and turns round in front of the rails, it is best to lead him up to them at the trot and let him go just in front of them. But also, at the start, you can lead a horse over the cavalletti.

With horses who really know cavalletti, the real trotting work can begin at once. The rider must try to regulate the trot cadence. Horses almost always become lazy as soon as they have got over the initial excitement. By clicking the tongue, or by short, sharp words or even by raising the lunge whip, the horse must be made to keep up a good active trot. Also, horses must be stopped from putting in little extra steps between the cavalletti instead of taking them in long, free strides. Sensitive horses require only the minimum driving; some, on the other hand, need a lot of encouragement. All horses are different. A quiet, understanding rider will not find it difficult to establish the right contact with his horse. Those who do not yet possess this feeling, can take this opportunity to practise and so gain experience for their future career in the saddle.

Phase 4: Increasing the distances between the cavalletti rails

Before the *distances* between the rails may be increased the horse should be made to execute a strong trot down the side of the school that is free of cavalletti and, by reducing the aid of the lunge whip, he should shorten to an ordinary trot.

The rails may be moved a few inches further apart only when this has been well executed. It is important that this should be done so carefully that the horse's action is not interrupted. In this way a smooth lengthening of stride leads to a well-marked strong trot.

How far the cavalletti may be gradually drawn apart, can only be decided with each individual horse. The greatest distance must not exceed 5 ft (1.5 m). The proper distance has been exceeded if the horse is forced to put in an extra stride.

Duration of the exercise

The length of *time* that this exercise may last is dependent upon the horse's condition. Because of the increased work, there will be – as we have seen in the first chapter – a greater demand on the muscles and joints. In my experience, 10 minutes is more than enough for a normal riding horse. In order to find out the right time, the rider will have to *observe* his horse *constantly* during schooling. Attention is particularly drawn to the liveliness of action, the facial expression, the play of the ears, position of tail and the movement of the nostrils in breathing. Sweating is not necessarily a sign of exhaustion, only if it is sudden or severe. Horses should not reach the point of sweating during schooling as they will lose condition.

If anyone is really interested, he will soon be in a position to judge. He will constantly find new characteristics in his horse and in a very short time will recognise when his horse is tired or when he is just trying it on. If there is any doubt, then it is probably tiredness, especially if the stride has lost its elasticity. Horses appreciate a kind word when they have carried out their work properly; if one movement after another is well done then let the horse walk and change direction but do not stop work or walk *past* the cavalletti because almost all horses will try to avoid them if they can.

After 10–20 minutes of preparation (including warming up, loose exercise, exercise in side-reins) a further 10 minutes over the cavalletti, and finally 5–10 minutes increasing the pace, the training period comes to an end. The side-reins are removed. The horse is then quietly walked about until he has dried off and the flanks and nostrils are no longer heaving. Then he may be taken to the stable.

It only remains to decide how often this work is to be carried out. Those who have time to exercise their horses daily, should let them go free over ground rails every 8 to 14 days. In addition to this, ride over the cavalletti a number of times; further details are to be found in the Appendix.

For those who cannot work their horses regularly it is still a good idea to use the ground rails every so often. The horse improves with every single lesson that is systematically worked out. For this reason alone the use of ground rails is recommended, even if no uniform progress is guaranteed. Obviously these alone cannot achieve the equivalent of methodical schooling.

Horses who are going to be used for a special task, require a corresponding *special training*. Three-day event (Olympic trial) horses who are required to have great stamina for the cross-country section, can for example, be kept in condition by regular work at the trot over cavalletti. I always do this and have been quite successful. I add cavalletti work three or four times a week, so that the length of time spent in schooling is sometimes increased by 50–70 minutes. During the winter, condition can be maintained by frequent trotting over cavalletti.

On the lunge

The advantage of lungeing a horse over ground rails lies in the fact that stiffness in the neck and quarters can be eliminated. Through the position of the horse's body on the circle, the inside muscles are contracted and the outside neck and back muscles are stretched. The inside hind foot has to take more weight. The length of the stride can be changed or altered as required by making the circle larger or smaller without altering the cavalletti. This is a worthwhile advantage because after every extension one can get the horse's stride back into the normal length and the ordinary cadence.

The trainer has to pay attention all

the time to be able to lunge his horse correctly over ground rails. The horse has to be secure between lunge line and whip. If you are even slightly inattentive, the long lunge line can be caught on the cavalletti stands. You must keep the horse on a true circle, otherwise his stride will increase or decrease the moment he leaves the circle. So the rider has got to be 'on the mark'. I would recommend to beginners to let their horses go free over the cavalletti at the start, or else to ride over them. It is easier to lunge if one uses a single cavalletto or spreads them singly round the circle. Only by using rails on square supports (see page 18) is it possible to avoid catching the lunge line.

Building the cavalletti

From my own experience the illustration (on page 29) shows the best use of the cavalletti on a circle, because it does not need to be changed during the lesson. But of necessity it does mean that horses must be used to cavalletti work and can therefore be asked to take on a number of ground rails.

The centre circle is for lungeing, the right hand circle is for trotting work and the left hand circle for work at the walk. The outsides of both circles should have wings for safety. If you do not possess eight cavalletti then six are enough – three a side, with perhaps an extra pole placed on the ground between the cavalletti. But three a side are quite enough. It is important that the rails should radiate from the circle so that the cadence of the movement may be maintained.

For the trot, the distance in the centre of the rails must be 4 ft 3 in (1.3 m) so that there is sufficient distance for an increase or decrease of stride. At the walk, the rails should be 2 ft 8 in (0.8 m) apart at their centres. I do not recommend the use of cavalletti in this exercise at the canter because it seems to me that the danger of injury through the increased speed is needless, taking into account the small advantage attained. (I do think it is a good idea to canter horses on the lunge over small obstacles. However this does not belong to cavalletti work but to proper training in jumping.) The reasons against letting the horse work at the walk, when going free in the school are not valid when he is on the lunge. When he is on the lunge, with the aid of the line, the use of the whip and the rider's voice he can be easily kept up to the proper cadence of the walk.

Phase 1: Lungeing without cavalletti

Before the horse can be lunged over cavalletti, he has first to learn to lunge properly. It should never be forgotten that horses who get an hour's exercise daily may have to spend twenty-three hours in their boxes. Therefore they should have at least a few minutes in which to enjoy themselves without constraint. Most horses go off at a gallop and probably buck as well. All you need to do is to try to quieten them with your voice to get them back to a normal cadence. You can 'play' the lunge line, by shortening or giving but keep the whip *still* under the arm. There are also horses who have to be driven right from the start and they can be stopped after only a few rounds.

Phase 2: Adjusting the side-reins and fastening the lunge line

After changing the rein and lungeing in the opposite direction, the side-reins can be attached. Remember that the horse is to go on a circle and that the inside rein must be shorter than the outside. The correct length will be about 2–4 in (5–10 cm) – about three to six holes shorter. The function of the outside rein is to control the inner bend and to prevent evasion through the outside shoulder. The outside rein must therefore complement the inner rein. Side-reins are fastened, as for work on a

Layout of cavalletti for lunge work.

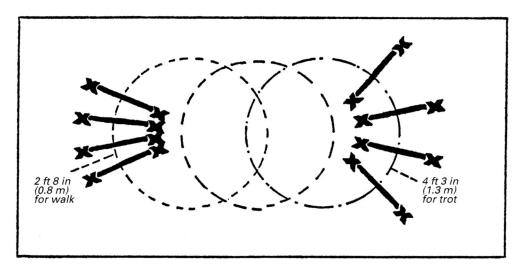

2 ft 8 in
(0.8 m)
for walk

4 ft 3 in
(1.3 m)
for trot

straight line, to the girth under the saddle flap, so that the horse may stretch his neck forwards and downwards. Therefore the length of the reins is adjustable, so that they may be altered during the lesson as required. Through the progression of working the horse loose, then with side-reins and then over cavalletti, one acquires a much softer connection with the horse's mouth. With the side-reins, the bit cannot be pulled through the horse's

Lungeing without cavalletti. The lunge line should not be so slack.

mouth sideways. The other option is to fix the lunge line to the bridle (connection being to a strap between the snaffle rings).

A third possibility is to put the lunge line through the inside snaffle ring and to fix it to the outside ring, so that the horse's chin tends to face outwards. This can be rather strong and can cause the horse to go on the circle with an outside bend.

The strongest way of fixing the lunge line is to put it through the inside ring, over the head of the horse and then fix it on the outside ring, but this option is not recommended.

If a cavesson is used, the lunge line will be attached to the cavesson and not to the inside bit ring, so that the bit cannot be pulled out of the horse's mouth.

When the reins have been adjusted there can follow a few exercises on the centre circle. With the driving influence of the lunge whip and the voice the horse will lower his neck at the trot and canter and will confidently accept the bit. Trot to canter changes on the middle circle are beneficial. When this has been attained after 10–15 minutes on both reins, the first lesson over the cavalletti may begin.

Phase 3: Lungeing over cavalletti

The first thing to do is to accustom the young horse to ground rails. So a single rail is put in front of him and he is allowed to go over it several times in his own way. As soon as he has got over his initial fear, more cavalletti are added until the required number has been reached. Begin at the trot since horses usually accelerate of their own accord, and finish with walking exercise. After a short pause, which gives one the chance to praise the horse and to re-adjust the side-reins in order to change direction, the lesson is

Attaching the lunge line.
Above left: to the inside snaffle ring.
Below left: to a strap connecting the two bit rings.
Above right: through the inside snaffle ring to the outside bit ring.
Below right: to the bridle and the snaffle ring.

continued on the other rein. Now he should be asked without further delay to go over several cavalletti.

With horses who already know cavalletti work, one can use the arrangement of cavalletti (on page 29) right from the start. As soon as the horse has been worked on the centre circle the lungeing circle will be extended to the outside circle. There is a *difficulty* here. Right from the start you must succeed in getting the horse placed in the centre of the cavalletti, so that he finds the best position. If the horse is presented out of step at his very first try, then he may well lose his confidence, and the trainer will have considerable difficulty in getting him into a quiet, supple stride.

How should one *increase the circle*? By letting the lunge line slip through the fingers and by directing the whip in the direction of the shoulder. It helps to walk a few steps towards the horse so that he moves out. It is also a help to let the line 'snake' a little, so that the horse moves away from it. Increasing the circle should first be practised on the centre circle a few times, before you let the horse take the cavalletti. Then the actual lesson at the trot can begin.

Care must be taken here, because the horse's inside hind foot has to take on more work. You must watch your horse's movements very carefully: if he treads unevenly after clearing the ground rails it points to stress, possibly pain, in the muscles, and this means a return to the centre circle. Even without any sign of stress, I suggest returning to the centre circle after he has cleared the cavalletti five to eight times, before taking up the lesson again. The continual *change* between the centre circle and clearing the rails both at the walk and trot, makes the horse handy and works the muscles.

Also this avoids the monotony that takes away the horse's pleasure in his work and after all, his entire education and training rests on this pleasure.

Even if you have to overcome a one-sided stiffness you must not forget the *change of rein*. I have noticed that horses relax more easily after a pause and change of rein than if you keep on working at the more difficult side.

The outer side of the cavalletti circle, where the distances are longer, may only be used when the trainer has acquired sufficient experience and skill.

If the right treatment is used, in due course the *contact between horse and trainer* will become very close. The horse will need less and less help and in the end one is surprised how easily he can be controlled, as soon as he has acquired confidence. Then work becomes a real pleasure and this is a great help for one's future riding career.

Duration of the exercise

Lungeing over cavalletti should never last longer than 20 minutes, so that the entire lesson takes up the time as follows: 10 minutes at the walk, 5–10 minutes without side-reins, 10–15 minutes with side-reins fastened but without using the rails and 20 minutes at the trot and walk over the rails. At the finish the horse is worked at the walk without side reins, until he has dried off and can be taken back to his box. I do not recommend more than one such lesson every eight to fourteen days because the exercise over ground rails has to be included within the whole training programme and if carried out more often would prove to be too strenuous for the horse. Further details regarding training methods will be found in the Appendix.

*Lungeing over cavelletti with the correct
tension on the lunge line and good whip
position.*

Cavalletti work with Horse and Rider on Straight Lines

Cavalletti work with Horse and Rider on Straight Lines

In spite of the help obtained with and without the lunge line, the biggest difficulty of training begins once the rider is mounted. All the work that has gone before has the common aim of laying the foundation stone for future equitation, and should also be a valuable help to the rider for his own influence in the saddle. Once mounted, we have to make the most of everything we have learned. The many possibilities of more advanced education must be made clear to both horse and rider and all work must be so consolidated that they are able to carry out even difficult exercises with ease.

The basis for this is to be able to ride over cavalletti *on a straight line*.

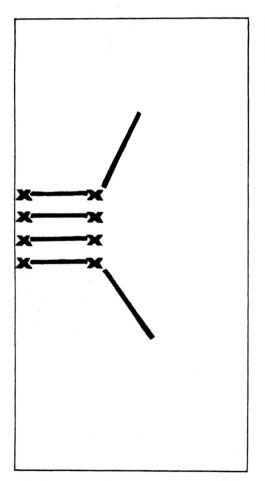

Layout of cavalletti on the track.

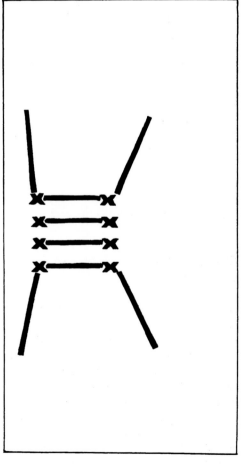

Layout of cavalletti beside the track.

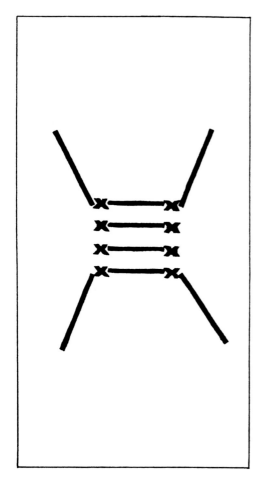

Layout of cavalletti on the centre line.

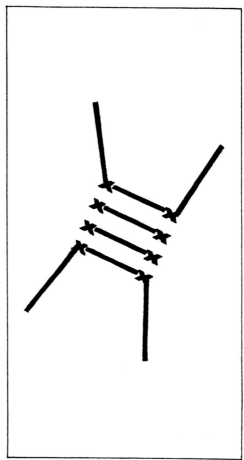

Layout of cavalletti on the diagonal.

Different ways of arranging cavalletti

Before every lesson one must think over carefully what one hopes to achieve during that particular hour and then choose the type of cavalletti for this. In my opinion there are five ways of building cavalletti in a straight line for this work. They are as follows.

The simplest arrangement is to erect several cavalletti one after the other close to the wall of a long side of the school, or – in the open – close to the side of the outdoor arena, measured out for the proper stride. The advantage is that the horse can keep to the track and therefore will not so easily try to run out sideways. The rider can then pay less attention to his horse and more to his own seat. To begin with, this is the way that horses and riders with little experience get themselves accustomed to using ground rails.

A somewhat more difficult arrangement is cavalletti that are erected inwards beside the track. They have the advantage that one does not need to ride over them every time round but they also require one to turn off the track. To make

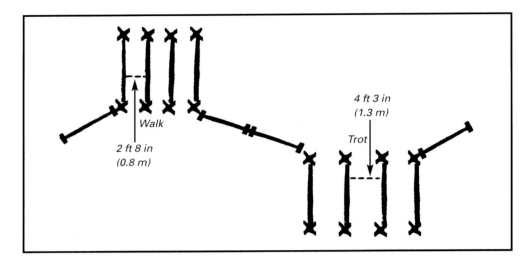

Layout of cavalletti for trot and walk combined: beside the track (above); beside the centre line (below).

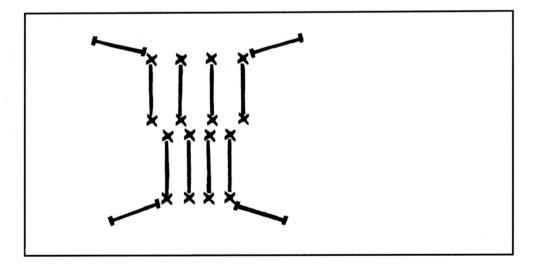

this a little easier, wings can be added to the sides. Older horses will not require such precautionary measures. In the same way, wings can be waived if one wants to give young riders on older horses a problem to execute, to turn their horses from the track and to ride over the wingless cavalletti.

The erection of cavalletti on the centre line requires only a slight deviation. I find this well worthwhile because it offers the opportunity to change the rein/direction, by using the length of the school and so ride over these obstacles.

To ride over cavalletti on the diagonal requires a lot more concentration. In my experience it is very difficult to ride straight, and I have never enjoyed it, because it is not easy to erect ground rails exactly at right angles to the proposed diagonal line. But because it is more difficult, I do recommend this arrangement especially as an exercise of skill for young riders on older horses.

Those who are really anxious to see their horses progress will build cavalletti for both the trot and the walk since this eliminates the tiresome business of stopping to alter rails during the lesson. It is then really a matter of preference whether they are erected beside the track or near the centre line.

Finally, it is the trainer's business during the course of the lessons to build the right system of cavalletti for each of his pupils and for each horse. An experienced trainer accepts this as a matter of course.

Cavalletti work at the walk on a loose rein

The *first mounted exercise* over ground rails is executed at the walk because this is the gait in which horses have the most confidence when ridden. One commences with one cavalletto and allows the horse a free rein. Aids are used only to keep the horse going forward. If necessary the voice should be used to keep up impulsion. At the second attempt horses usually go of their own accord and need scarcely any help. The upper part of the rider's body must be inclined a little in the forward position so that he does not come down on the horse's back if he should jump. If the horse accepts this quite calmly then a second rail can be put up at a distance of about 2 ft 8 in–3 ft 3 in (0.8 m–1 m), then a third and so on,

Walk over cavalletti on a loose rein: a 5-year-old Trakehner stallion ridden by Ingrid Klimke. He is curious, confident and completely relaxed.

until the required number has been reached – but not more than six. I have often found that horses become excitable once they see several ground rails one after the other but they soon quieten down if I take away one or two cavalletti. In these cases the increase was too sudden but after a short time all the rails could be replaced.

If the horse is already used to ground rails, then the complete set can be put up right from the start. For the first few times the reins should be free. The horse must feel free to learn to balance himself. If he walks evenly over the individual obstacles then the distance between is correct; otherwise the distance must be corrected.

An even stride over ground rails strengthens the natural hoof beat of the walk. As we know, at this gait, each foot is placed separately on the ground as follows:

1. Off fore foot
2. Near hind foot
3. Near fore foot
4. Off hind foot

Any deviation is faulty, especially the amble, when the four-time movement is so hurried that the beats one and four and two and three almost fall together. But I have never actually seen a horse trying to go over ground rails at the amble. All horses seem to find their natural gait.

With the correct aids the rider will be able to improve on each movement. We differentiate between the medium walk, the collected walk and the extended walk. The *medium walk* must be executed with the horse feeling the bit and yielding at the poll. So it can happen that the required length of stride is shortened. At the medium walk the hind feet must reach over the tracks of the forefeet. This extension or overtracking can be encouraged by working the horse over ground rails because the correct distances demand

Medium walk on the bit. The horse has a good head position. The rider's upper body is a little behind the movement.

Medium walk on the bit. Rider and horse in balance.

this length of stride. With this end in view, the rider gets his horse on the bit by careful pushing with his back and thighs and a gentle feeling of the horse's mouth through the reins with his hands. As soon as the horse drops his neck and extends willingly on the reins, cavalletti work can begin. The hands should be low. About a length in front of the obstacle, the rider will give to the horse's mouth so that the horse feels in no way constrained. To make it easier, the rider's body will incline slightly forward. Then, *correctly* ridden, the horse will stride over the rails with lowered nose and relaxed back muscles.

Of course it is not always easy to get the horse to lower his head and accept the bit. Some horses stiffen their necks and their backs and refuse to go on the bit. In this and similar cases the following correction has proved valuable. The horse is turned in a circle/volte or a figure of eight in front of the cavalletti then, with well-timed aids at the turn, the horse is presented again straight at the cavalletti. Just in front or over the rails let him feel the bit (feel the reins so that he chews the bit). Usually the horse then goes freely forward, drops his head to see where he is going and so relaxes all his back muscles. Every well-executed exercise should be rewarded by patting him on the neck. Finally, the exercise will be repeated several times until it is successful.

The most important points for the rider to watch for are:

1. **To ride straight**
2. **To keep impulsion**
3. **Neck low and accepting the bit lightly and hands held low**
4. **To let the upper part of the body go with the movement of the horse**

Faulty seat at walk over cavalletti

a) Off balance and not straight.

b) Leaning too far forward, reins useless.

c) Leaning too far back, interfering with the horse's mouth, hands too high.

The horse will be brought out of his cadence if you ride carelessly or place him at an angle in front of the cavalletti because the distance at a slant between the rails is obviously greater. Careless presentation leads to 'creeping' and does not teach the horse to walk properly. A sudden yielding or giving of the reins just in front of the cavalletti only upsets the horse and prevents his free forward movement. On the other hand a heavy-handed grasp on the reins with a stiff back, will disturb the horse's back muscles. In order not to lose impulsion in front of the cavalletti, I suggest that the upper part of the rider's body should be forward rather than backward because, with the latter, it is impossible to lift the weight in time over the obstacle. Both voice and heels help impulsion. If a whip is carried then it should be used lightly on the shoulder; if used behind the saddle or even on the croup, the rider's weight/seat goes back too easily.

The stride of the *extended walk* exceeds that of the medium walk. The hind foot is placed far over the track of the fore foot. The rider gives his horse freedom of the neck but without losing complete contact with the mouth. Without the use of cavalletti there is always the danger that impulsion intended to increase the length of stride, will result only in the stride becoming shorter and more hurried. By the correct spacing of the cavalletti this can be overcome as they are placed wider apart little by little. At the very latest, I recommend letting the horse feel the bit over the first rail so that he may be encouraged to extend himself as much as possible.

The distances between the rails is regulated to the size of the horse, from about 2 ft 8 in to 3 ft–3 ft 4 in (0.8 to 1–1.1 m). As soon as the horse tries to put in extra steps, then the correct distance has been exceeded. The only

exception to this is carelessness on the part of the horse, when instead of trying to work properly he may put in an extra step. In this case, at the next attempt, the rider must produce more impulsion. Since this exercise 'extended walk over cavalletti' puts a great strain on muscles, tendons and ligaments it should not be practised more than about ten to fifteen times.

For the *collected walk* the distances between the rails will be shortened to 2 ft 8 in (0.8 m) or less. The stride of this gait is so short that the horse's hind foot falls just short of the track of the fore foot. The single steps must be higher and more impressive. The horse's neck is raised, and the forehead and nose approach the perpendicular. The collected walk is one of the most difficult exercises in dressage. Over and over again one sees hurried, short steps executed in a sort of amble. The reason for this is easily explained. Horses are spurred into activity but are none the less meant to achieve a shorter stride. In order to make them do this, the reins must be shortened. If the horse has misunderstood his rider, he walks faster instead of higher and loses the hoof beat of the walk. Many a good dressage rider has failed because of this problem – so I use cavalletti to help me out. A horse cannot hurry his steps over ground rails, because he has to step higher than usual to get over them. So the four-time hoof beat is assured. By taking hold of the bit and shortening the reins, it is up to the rider to obtain the proper position of the neck over ground rails. But it must also be remembered that definite results – as with all cavalletti exercises – are produced only during the actual stride over the cavalletti. Accordingly, continued success is not guaranteed and hopes should not be raised. Work over cavalletti simply serves to put the rider and horse on the right path. It creates the psychological and physiological

prerequisites for success, but it is left to the rider's horsemanship to make this success permanent.

According to the stage that the horse has reached in his schooling, it is recommend that the rails for the exercise 'collected walk' should be raised to the middle height of about 1 ft 2 in (35 cm). After repeating this about five to ten times, at the far side of the school, a turn about at the walk is completed by giving a free rein. Regarding timing, the collected exercises belong to the latter part of the lesson, whilst the medium and extended walk belong at the commencement.

Collected walk over cavalletti.

A useful preparation for both jumping and cross-country, is to ride over the ground rails at the trot, the rails being placed double the distance apart. In this exercise the horse learns to put in an extra stride. For this purpose one rail will be removed from the centre of the row, so that the horse takes one stride without a rail. His concentration is thereby

Walk over cavalletti on a loose rein: an experienced 7-year-old Holsteiner gelding completely relaxed and trusting his rider.

Medium walk on the bit correctly ridden.

Walk over cavalletti with one stride between the penultimate and last cavalletti: uneven distances.

increased. Horses learn to balance themselves and are taught to carry themselves safely over uneven ground. Surefootedness is most important in all horses.

To avoid the horse getting bored and to keep his attention it is a good idea to alternate between walk and trot. I generally consider it unnecessary to change the height of one or two ground rails, since horses can become suspicious. However, in special circumstances, perhaps with an inattentive horse, there may be a case for altering the height of one or two cavalletti in order to increase his attention.

It is quite obvious that horses may sometimes stumble during their work and lose their balance. You can be fairly certain that they will do this at the beginning, because balance has to be learnt and few horses are born clever. But there is no need to worry about this since the danger of falling is just as great when jumping and much more likely. Injuries are usually only caused by the careless erection of the cavalletti, the exercise lasting too long, or failure by the rider to give the horse the right aids. Occasional knocking of a rail by the feet or fetlock joint is not likely to cause damage and may be disregarded.

How often work at the walk over ground rails should be practised, is dependent upon the time the rider can spare. If he rides daily, once or twice a week during winter and once every eight to fourteen days the rest of the time should be about right; otherwise within definite periods. The inclusion of the complete system of cavalletti work can be found in the training system in the Appendix.

Cavalletti work at the trot

Those who began by riding at the walk over ground rails, are now so far prepared that they can commence to trot

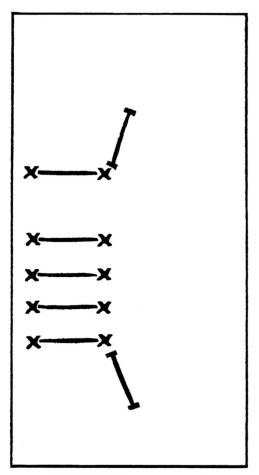

over several cavalletti – the arranging of which was described on page 20. Those who *start* with the trot, must begin with one obstacle, building up to four. The distance between is now 4 ft 3 in–4ft 10 in (1.3–1.5 m). The height remains at the lowest 6–8 in (15–20 cm).

While the walk is primarily for the horse's education, work at the trot is equally good for both *horse and rider*. In schooling, therefore, one has to differentiate between training the young horse and training the young rider on older horses. This division is necessary since I do not wish to create the impression that only young riders and young horses can be schooled over cavalletti, because, in my opinion, work over ground rails, as I showed in the chapter 'Theoretical Groundwork', is valuable for all riders and all horses whether they are beginners or more advanced.

Left: Cavalletti with one stride between penultimate and last cavalletti.

Below: Ingrid Klimke walking over cavalletti with one stride between. Medium walk on the bit with low hands and a strong seat supporting an extended neck.

Working trot over cavalletti, rising trot with one hand holding mane.

Ingrid Klimke trotting with the seat out of the saddle, inclining forward.

One of the best exercises for the *rider* is to trot – and later to canter – over cavalletti, as it helps to train him in the so-called forward seat. This seat is the most useful aid to the horse when jumping or going cross-country. The rider inclines the upper part of his body forward and puts his weight through his thighs and knees more to the horse's

Trotting over cavalletti with folded arms.

Ingrid Klimke working over cavalletti in trot standing in the stirrups.

flanks. The horse's back is eased. The rider's hands remain low and steady on both sides of the withers. The knees are firm to the sides and the heels down so that the correct position of the leg is ensured. The stirrups will be shortened two to four holes. All these points are well-known and may be found in every good instruction book. The question that

Rising trot with the correct seat and the horse accepting the bit.

is not so often answered is, how the forward seat may be learnt. This is our next point.

To begin with, as already stated, the stirrups are shortened two to four holes. Then the trot over the cavalletti will be practised in three different phases.

The *first exercise* is easy. Its only purpose is to help the rider's confidence and to overcome diffidence. At the rising trot the rider inclines slightly forwards as he approaches the ground rails; he may hold the mane in both hands. At the second attempt he will put one hand forward towards his horse's mouth and to finish, both hands forward, until he feels quite safe.

The *second exercise* is much more difficult. Its purpose is to increase the grip of the knees, and requires that the rider shall stand in his stirrups as he rides over the ground rails. Once again he holds on to the mane until he has learnt to keep his balance with a firm knee grip independently of the horse's movements. Little by little the hands are freed of the mane and put forward towards the

horse's mouth. He may keep contact lightly with the neck. When the rider has learnt to balance himself standing in the stirrups and to *go forward* smoothly with his horse, then the *third exercise* with the arms folded may be practised. This exercise is to teach the rider complete independence of his hands. The objective has been reached as soon as the upper part of the body remains in a perpendicular position during the rising trot over the cavalletti, and the hands remain still and do not move up and down with every movement of the upper body. Then and then only, is the rider able to prove that he has mastered the correct seat and has fulfilled the basic requirements for the canter and for jumping.

There is a further exercise to give the rider the feeling of basculation, or arching, of the horse's back and this is to *sit down* in the movement of the trot over cavalletti. This exercise is only for those

Active rising trot on the bit.

riders who have a strong resilient seat. When a rider is so far advanced that he can begin to feel the horse's movement, he can develop this feeling by *sitting down* over cavalletti; he will learn to feel when the horse bascules and is more easily ridden, and when he is stiff and throws the rider. If the rider does not *go with* his horse, the activity of the horse's back muscles will be disturbed and the rider will be in danger of spoiling his horse. Therefore the greatest care must be taken when riding in sitting trot over cavalletti. I recommend it only on experienced school horses or for a good rider who wants to teach his horse the passage – more about this later. The collected trot is the best cadence because one can sit down in the saddle better.

Schooling the horse to *trot* over cavalletti should begin with the working trot. The trot is a movement in two-time when both diagonal legs leave the ground together: the movements are working trot, collected trot, medium trot and extended trot. At the working trot the hind foot should step into the track of the forefoot. The horse should move freely, rhythmically and with expression. To ensure this, it is necessary that the horse's back should be supple and the movement coming from the hindquarters should flow forward to the forehand without interruption. The back muscles can be developed by the energetic action of the diagonal legs over the cavalletti. And the horse must be ridden at the sitting trot with extended neck and low head carriage. The lower the horse extends himself in the forward downward movement over the ground rails, the more he will arch his back. The best exercise to strengthen the back muscles is to let him take the bit over the cavalletti (see illustration on page 53). It is often more difficult to carry this out than one would think. It requires a lot of thought even to ride a horse in, in a quiet, even cadence with lowered and extended head carriage.

Collected trot, sitting. Distances between the cavalletti should be shortened to 4 ft–4 ft 4 in (1.2–1.3 m).

Working trot, sitting. The nose is slightly behind the vertical.

Lazy horses are fairly easily brought on by impulsion. Generally most horses quicken their pace as soon as they see the ground rails and try to canter. Here it is necessary to control the ordinary cadence with the half-halt and by taking and giving the reins to prevent the horse lifting his head or 'getting the bit between his teeth'. Because as soon as his head goes up, he will stiffen over the rails,

Working trot with a light contact.

A little above the bit.

losing his balance and may injure himself by stumbling or slipping. If he does not quieten down in a short time, then he must go back to work over a single rail.

A little head-raising, especially with sensitive horses, does not matter. Quite a number of horses raise their heads in front of obstacles or cavalletti simply because they want to see what lies in front of them. As they jump or go over

the ground rails they bring their heads down of their own accord and arch their backs at the same time. It would therefore be completely wrong if the rider tried to prevent his horse from raising his head at all. He would only encourage opposition and lose his horse's confidence in him.

On the other hand, if horses have stiff jaws and necks it may mean a sensitive back or that they resent the bit. Before they ever reach the cavalletti stage, such horses need a lot of skill to get them to accept the bit. They should be worked on the circle, in the volte and on serpentines to encourage them to submit. Only when this has been accomplished can they be shown how to lower their heads, to regulate their cadence and then to trot over cavalletti. One can quieten them by riding in and turning away or by doing a volte a few paces away from the ground rails and by halting and reining-back in front of the first obstacle. In such situations, which can only be indicated, because all horses

An experienced horse shows the way to a young horse. Ingrid Klimke on a 7-year-old Holstein gelding followed by Andreas Busacker on a 4-year-old Trakehner mare.

are different, it rests with the rider to exercise both patience and commonsense. Once you have obtained contact with your horse and have skilfully used it several times you will find that success is only a question of time. The rider will be astonished to see how his horse responds to him. After a few schooling lessons, the horse will allow himself to be ridden-in normally without showing any excitement. And the relaxing effect of working over the cavalletti will soon help to overcome any difficulties. Should the horse get agitated at a later point it shows that something is not right. Perhaps he has been asked to do too much and he is uncomfortable. The work should then either be stopped straight away, or less asked for, to finish on a good note.

Faulty riding in trot over cavalletti.
Top: Hands too high, upper body leaning
backwards, horse hollow-backed.
Right: Against the hand. The rider, although
leaning forward, is behind the movement and
his lower leg is too far forward.
Bottom: Too fast, the rider's lower leg is too
far forward and the horse is above the bit.

Cavalletti work in trot over uneven distances. Horse and rider are in balance, with the horse accepting the bit.

To recap, the problems that the rider has to watch for when riding over cavalletti are basically:

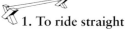

1. To ride straight
2. A quiet but not a lazy cadence
3. Lowered position of the neck with a light contact on the bit on a long rein, hands kept low
4. To go *with* the horse's movement with the upper part of the body, preferably at a sitting trot

Further, care must be taken in spite of an even cadence, that the horse does not 'creep' but treads with an unbroken, even stride. The *reins* should be too long rather than too short, so that the horse feels in no way constrained. Any kind of constraint in certain positions causes disquiet and opposition. Constant praise by patting the horse's neck makes him happy and willing.

After a successful exercise at the working trot the lesson can either be concluded or continued with the other movements at the trot. The *collected trot*, sitting, has already been described (page 51). It is expressed by an even, raised step, short stride and a pleasing raising of the neck. The medium trot is recognisable by the energetic longer stride covering more ground. The horse must extend himself and gain ground. For this purpose the cavalletti are gradually spaced from 4 ft 3 in–4 ft 10 in (1.3–1.5 m) apart. It is ridden at the sitting trot with a light rein feeling the horse's mouth. Two or three lengths in front of the rails the rider will increase the cadence to 'lengthen the stride'.

It is important that the speed to the cavalletti is uniformly increased because then the best extension can be reached. If the cadence is too free at the start then there is the danger of hurried movement. The horse stiffens, canters on or loses his rhythm through sudden shortening and then lengthening in front of the first obstacle.

The exercise 'lengthen stride' over cavalletti, requires an exact distribution of the cadence. The rider acquires the feeling for his horse's length of stride, is conscious when it harmonizes and schools his eye permanently for the correct distance. Accordingly this lesson is at the same time an excellent aid to jumping and cross-country riding.

The development of the maximum activity of the *extended trot* is the result of the systematic schooling of the medium trot over cavalletti. To avoid risk of injury I never ride the extended trot over cavalletti, and thus I ensure that my horses always enjoy their schooling.

On the other hand an exercise which I especially recommend preparatory to the *passage* is to put up the rails to about 14 in (35 cm) and to ride over them at the collected trot. Obviously this schooling is only suitable for advanced horses under experienced riders.

I am quite sure that this suggestion will be disputed because those few riders who are in a position to teach their horses the passage already have doubts about the use of cavalletti for dressage horses. They would certainly refuse to use ground rails to teach the passage. I can only answer by saying that unfortunately many dressage riders think too much about practising school movements such as travers, change of leads at the canter, pirouette

In rising trot over cavalletti but the horse is not straight so there is a danger of the horse losing his balance.

etc. and are thereby in danger of forgetting the *aim of dressage*, which is to make the horse more beautiful and stronger by systematic gymnastics and simply to improve his natural action. How often with dressage horses that are being ridden-in, does one miss that easing-off with a dropped nose to relax the back muscles. One is therefore not

Moving quicker over cavalletti to lengthen the stride.

Lengthening the stride in trot with cadence, keeping the horse together but so that his nose does not come behind the vertical.

Passage steps over cavalletti.

surprised to see horses with such shaky action that they are scarcely able to jump a low obstacle at the conclusion of the dressage test. Moreover it would not help at all to use cavalletti for the first time to help with the passage. Because if horses have not basically learnt to move freely, when they see cavalletti later, at best they will become excitable and awkward. The

same thing applies to those riders who have never had a basic training over cavalletti. I too, used to be mistrustful of using cavalletti to help with the passage, but this was simply because I was worried that the horses would hurt their legs. However my worries proved to be without foundation, because that kind of injury never happened. Nevertheless I must add that, within limits, special care must be taken and there must be intervals of rest during schooling. In any case it is worthwhile trying this work since one reaches one's objective quicker and there is the guarantee that the horse's hind legs will move actively and evenly. Special points of the exercise can only be discovered by the ability of the rider, from case to case. The maximum of four cavalletti placed one after the other must in no circumstances be exceeded.

As described for the walk, the horse's attention at trot can be increased by arranging cavalletti with one stride between. One rail is removed out of the line, so that a blank space remains. The distance of 4 ft 3 in (1.3 m) conforms with the normal working cadence. It is the rider's job to create sufficient impulsion to obtain an even trot over the rails. The one stride in between must not be shorter, otherwise the horse will lose his rhythm and will stumble. The schooling at the trot over ground rails is timed to follow schooling at the walk. The length of the exercise corresponds or is adjusted to the horse's stage of training and what is to be asked of him. About 15–20 minutes at the trot with short rests in between is normal. If the horse is being conditioned, then the period can be lengthened little by little to 30–35 minutes. More will be found in the training programme in the Appendix.

Rising trot with straight back. Rider and horse in complete harmony.

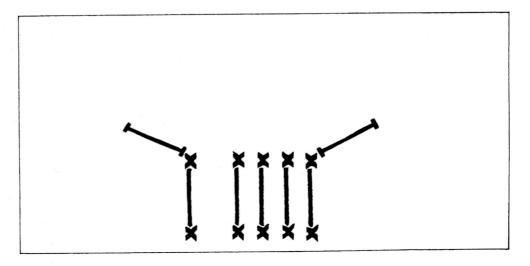

Cavalletti with one stride between, spaced for trot.

Cavalletti work at the canter

Riding at the canter over ground rails is the same as jumping over low obstacles that are placed at given distances one after the other. The canter is the horse's fastest school gait. One differentiates between the canter to the right or to the left, according to the side on which the horse's foreleg is leading. The gait has a three-time beat. The fourth phase finishes with a slight pause – the so-called *phase of suspension*, the period when the horse is momentarily suspended with all four legs in the air. The *movement of the canter* is therefore as follows:

1. Off hind leg
2. Near hind leg and off foreleg
3. Near foreleg
4. Period of suspension
(left canter)

At the gallop the second phase comes separately, so that a four-time beat may be heard. Otherwise the movements of the canter are divided into: collected, working, medium and extended canter. If the beat is lost, which constantly happens in the false shortened canter, then one calls it a faulty four-time canter which has the following hoof beats:

1. Off hind leg
2. Near hind leg
3. Off foreleg
4. Near foreleg
(left canter)

The correctly executed canter, however, is marked by an animated stride with a clearly marked suspension. Thus the proper *canter stride* is produced and it is only this that makes the movement animated and attractive.

A jump over an obstacle is simply a longer, higher canter stride. Therefore it is obvious that by using ground rails at the canter, it is a great help for jumping and cross-country. The main thing is to erect the cavalletti very carefully. In my experience the best height is about 1 ft 8 in (50 cm). The two lower heights are generally not treated very seriously by horses. The jump at the canter remains flat and extends forwards. Horses only go faster and are more impetuous, instead of being quieter and paying more attention, so that there is scarcely any chance of successful schooling. On the other hand, if the height is 1 ft 8 in

(50 cm), horses have to jump properly. For this reason it is enough if three cavalletti are used. The distance between them is about 11 ft (3.5 m) but the size and action of each individual horse must be taken into consideration.

As for the trot, schooling over ground rails is equally good for both horse *and* rider. And for this reason they are to be treated separately so that the various crucial points in the schooling may be recognised.

As far as the rider is concerned it means the completion of the *forward seat* which he has already practised at the trot. If possible it would be as well to use a schooled horse for this purpose. If the stirrups have not already been taken up, they should be shortened by two to four holes. Training will be divided practically into different stages since only a gradual – step by step – increase in all that is being demanded of the horse can ensure success. The quickest and surest way to achieve our objective is always by a systematic build-up.

Rising trot over cavalletti with one stride between. An obedient horse accepting the aids and using his back.

Using low cavalletti for canter work is useless for training.

Phase 1: Preparation for the forward seat at the canter

The exercise 'canter over cavalletti' will be practised at the canter in the forward seat on both reins. Horse and rider must have the opportunity to get used to this seat when cantering.

The proper way to take the weight off the saddle must be learnt. It requires a lot of practise to master it – especially at the beginning – because one can get cramp in the legs and back. Some horses also become excitable when their riders lean forward to take the weight out of the saddle. So it is very advisable to canter round the school a few times on both reins, without using the cavalletti. Beginners may find it useful to practise bending forwards from the hips preparatory to jumping and to let their hands go forwards with the reins.

Phase 2: Canter over cavalletti set at a distance of 11 ft (3.5 m)

The first exercise, to canter over cavalletti spaced at 11 ft (3.5 m) apart, may begin as soon as the horse has got used to a light feeling on the bit at a working cadence. One need not begin with a single rail because the horse has already gained confidence over ground rails when he was

Cavalletti distances for canter. For these cavalletti: distance 11 ft (3.5 m), height 1 ft 6 in (0.5 m)

11 ft (3.5 m)   11 ft (3.5 m)

With higher cavalletti the canter is better.

ridden at the walk and trot. If only two cavalletti are erected then there is a danger that he will try to jump both together – so a double distance is always chosen. The exercise with three cavalletti has as its objective to improve the rider's seat over a jump. From a working canter the rider will turn his horse straight towards the ground rails. He will use only enough impulsion to cause the horse to accept the bit. After that he will quietly prepare himself to incline at the hips and to place his hands forwards preparatory to the first jump without losing contact with his horse. Over the obstacle the rider assumes the jumping seat, which is characterized as follows:

1. Hands low and forwards towards the horse's mouth
2. To go with the horse through an easy inclination forward with the body
3. Legs straight and close to the horse's sides, heels down and knees gripping

The difficulty of this exercise lies in going with the movement of the horse three times as he jumps. Since the horse's jump follows in the same rhythm, the rider is thus able to concentrate on his position. If anyone is afraid that he may not go with his horse as he jumps then he should hold on to the mane. Even after a few attempts he will have gained so much *confidence* that he will be able to keep his hands free. Now the goal of the second schooling phase has been achieved.

Phase 3: Hands on hips

The third phase is a little test of courage. It demands that the rider leaves the reins free, puts his hands on his hips and canters over the ground rails. But the exercise is probably much easier than one expects. The reins are tied and placed on the horse's neck. With one hand the rider holds on to the knotted end, he then rides at a sitting trot on a circle and canters towards the enclosed side. Naturally this exercise can only be done on well-schooled 'schoolmaster' horses, who are lazy rather than impetuous. If the horse is quiet at the preliminary canter, the rider lets him canter straight on, on the track. As soon as he is sure that the horse is going to take the ground rails, he puts his hands on his hips. As he goes over the cavalletti he inclines his body forward as he did for jumping.

Riders are sometimes very hesitant about putting their hands on their hips. A number would have liked to refuse and only obeyed because they did not want to appear cowardly in front of their friends. But after their very first effort without holding the reins, they had changed their minds. They had discovered that this exercise is not so difficult and they were then anxious to repeat it. Their reluctance soon disappeared, and in place of it there appeared a smooth 'going with' the movement of the horse. There is much truth in the Russian proverb:

'Throw your heart over the wall, your horse will jump after it.'

Phase 4: Canter over cavalletti set at odd distances apart

The growing feeling of confidence achieves the necessary freedom and independence of the seat to influence the horse. When this point has been reached, a further exercise can be practised, and this is to school the rider's eye for the proper stride for jumping. For this purpose the third rail will be spaced at double the distance – at 21 ft (7 m) – behind the first two rails. The horse must now put in an extra canter stride as is frequently required of him when jumping double fences. One allows about 10 ft 6 in (3.5 m) for a stride so that the correct distance is measured from the number that may be required: 11 ft

(3.5 m); 34 ft (10.5 m); 45 ft 6 in (14 m) etc. If a third or fourth rail is erected at any one of these distances, then you are certain to have found the horse's correct stride. The rider then has only to follow the rhythm of the canter movement and to try to notice how many canter strides are needed to cover the ground. If he possesses the ability and an eye for distance he will develop the art of placing his horse. He will be able to judge from a distance if his horse can take the obstacle at the correct stride or not.*

For really experienced riders the exercise can be made even more difficult, in that the distance to the third rail is shortened to 32 ft (10 m) or increased to 35 ft 9 in (11 m). By this means the *lengthening forwards* as well as the *taking in and shortening* of a stride in restricted combinations, can be practised. We can now see how work over cavalletti gives the rider the entire basis for schooling over obstacles. Those who have learnt the proper jumping seat and to judge the correct distance of stride for the canter jump over ground rails, have mastered the ABC of jumping, and can outdistance their less thorough friends.

With regard to the length of time taken for this exercise, it must be understood that a lot more energy is needed at the canter to jump over a rail at 1 ft 8 in (50 cm) than the same work at the trot. Therefore schooling over three rails at a distance of 11 ft (3.5 m) should *not exceed more than five or six times* consecutively; schooling at odd distances over ground rails should *not exceed eight to ten times* in any one lesson.

Those who are primarily concerned with the training of the *horse* should observe the following:

* *Translator's note:* Nine times out of ten, horses hit fences because the rider's judgement and timing are wrong *and not because the horse is at fault.* This failure on the part of riders can be observed at any of the big shows, including Wembley.

Showjumpers and cross-country horses learn to jump the in-and-out [distance 11 ft (3.5 m)] through the first exercise; this is not often required of showjumpers but almost always of cross-country horses. The immediate take-off again after landing demands strength, handiness and confidence. The horse must extend himself and arch his back. Very often at the beginning horses are frightened of this obstacle (problem) especially if the second fence is not easily seen. This fear can be removed by cantering over cavalletti. Horses who have been cantered over ground rails at a quiet working cadence and with the correct help from the forward seat, soon gain confidence and realize that there is nothing difficult in jumping an in-and-out. If a horse is inclined to be overhasty, I recommend that he should not be given too much distance in front of the obstacle. The longer the distance, the more horses will pull. To be able to judge the correct distance is obviously essential. I have found that it pays to ride those horses naturally endowed with plenty of energy, so that they have only two or three canter strides straight to the cavalletti. Lazy horses, on the other hand, must be given sufficient space so that one can work up impulsion and not allow them to refuse.

Schooling at odd distances has proved useful, if one has to stop a horse 'taking hold' after jumping. Quite a number of young horses behave themselves in front of an obstacle, but they take the opportunity given during the act of jumping, so that as soon as they land they can suddenly increase their speed. Possibly the natural urge to gallop away from danger plays a role here.

This fear can be overcome if a third or fourth rail always at either 21 ft 6 in (7 m) or 31 ft (10.5 m) is erected. Horses then pay attention and look at the next obstacle. Then if the rider sits still and rides a large circle at the finish, it is generally possible to control the cadence of the working canter.

Only when the horses have learnt to jump the cavalletti at an even working canter, can one finish with *increasing* the distances and thereby demanding an earlier take-off, or shortening the distances which requires jumping from the hocks. Even greater success can be achieved by gymnastic jumping, and we shall discuss this in due course.

The schooling value of working dressage horses at the canter over cavalletti is too trifling to be worth the trouble. From the point of view that the very act of jumping a rail is simply a longer and higher canter stride, one could assume that riding over ground rails at the canter is a good way of improving the canter stride. But this assumption is mistaken. At the dressage canter the horse's forehand must move forward and upward whilst the hindquarters, with lowered croup, are used in active impulsion. When jumping over ground rails the hindquarters are similarly projected upwards. Thus the movement of the canter is different from that required by the dressage rider. The dressage rider can therefore give up the idea of schooling the canter over ground rails. Besides, work over cavalletti at the trot and walk is sufficient for this branch of equitation. If anyone wants to make a change in routine by jumping, then he should ride over single jumps.

To complete our observations it should be said that work over cavalletti at the canter comes at the end of the schooling period, inasmuch as it is not simply used as preparation for gymnastic jumping. Even in this case, work may only begin if the horse is thoroughly relaxed in all three gaits. As a method of getting the horse into condition, cantering over ground rails is simply not on because it uses up far too much energy. The integration of this type of schooling into a programme will be found in the Appendix.

Cavalletti Work on Circles and Half Circles

Cavalletti Work on Circles and Half Circles

The use of ground rails on circles makes a welcome change for young riders. As far as the horse is concerned, it is obvious that he must be already properly schooled over cavalletti on straight lines. Horses who have not learnt to go straight, will experience difficulties in balancing themselves at the turns. for example one can see this with young horses who are being cantered into the corners of the riding school. In order to control himself properly at the turn and in a confined space, the horse must first have learnt to put his hind feet exactly in the tracks of the forefeet. It is just the ability to do this which gives the horse his balance on circles. In all turns (or circles) the horse shall certainly be bent to the inside but, in himself, he must always be going straight. The horse has to be straightened through working on straight and curved lines so that the hind legs follow the same line as the front. If the horse is not straight, the hind legs do not follow the forelegs and the horse will move on two tracks and will lose the centre of balance. When turning, the horse should be turned slightly to the inside but basically remain straight.

Cavalletti work on circles should help if the horse is stiff on one side and make him more supple on both reins.

If a horse is not straight he often loses rhythm when turning but working on circles in rhythm and with light steps eliminates that.

When working over poles on the ground the horse has hardly any opportunity to let his hindquarters fall out. The distance between the poles helps the horse to keep his natural rhythm. There

Sitting trot over cavalletti on a circle, on left rein. An expressive movement in full control.

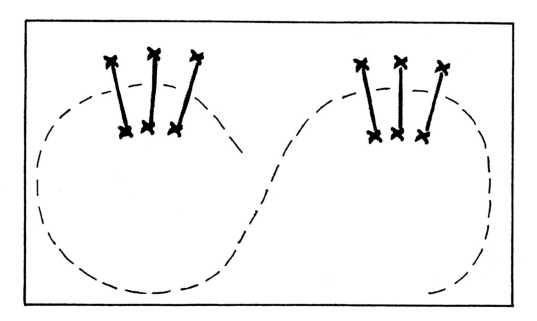

Placement of cavalletti on curved lines

is no time for the hindquarters to fall out.

Therefore if anyone is trying to eliminate a one-sided stiffness in the horse's neck or poll, or in his sides or hindquarters, he must be careful to prevent an evasion to the side with the hind feet following a different track from the forefeet. Horses who evade in this manner very soon lose their activity and are inclined not to submit to the rider and to go crookedly. When using cavalletti on a circle, both the actual step and the stride are so prescribed by the position of the rails, that horses keep the natural rhythm

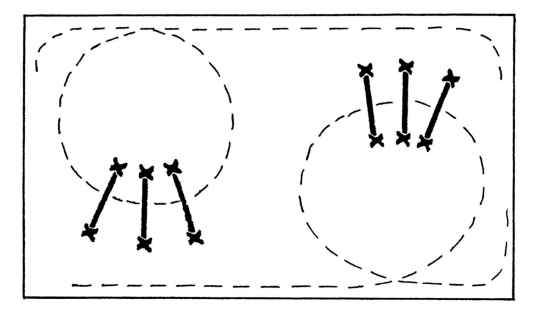

of their movement. There is little time for evasion from the tracks of the forefeet.

I recommend principally two different layouts of cavalletti. The *circular* layout has already been mentioned in the context of work on the lunge. To avoid repetition, I refer to the explanation given (see page 28). At the same time, use of the serpentine has proved worthwhile (see page 69). The idea is to use alternate reins and to make both sides of the horse supple. For this reason three cavalletti on each circle will be placed radiating from the track on the long side of the school, that is, either on both of the long sides of the school or all six cavalletti down one side. But it is most important that the track is kept free, so that one can ride outside using the entire school.

The exercise will be ridden at the trot with continual change out of the circle. To ride at the canter would take too much out of the horse and require too much skill since the horse normally changes the

Placement of cavalletti for work on straight lines and circles.

canter lead over every obstacle. As far as schooling is concerned, there is not much value to be had out of doing it at the walk, although in the case of a difficult horse one can first ride at this gait and then later go on to the trot.

Since riding over cavalletti on circles is very demanding and especially since the inside hind foot has to do most of the work, injuries can be caused by every false or too lengthy use of this method of schooling. Therefore one must always first consider carefully if the horse's training is sufficiently advanced to allow one to ride him over rails on the circle. If this question can honestly be answered in the affirmative, then I suggest that the exercise should be divided into the following phases.

Phase 1: Suppling exercises

The *first phase* serves as a preparation. It consists of suppling exercises in all three gaits and one or two exercises at the trot over ground rails on a straight line. After this there must be a short rest during which the cavalletti will be reorganised in circles or on a serpentine. If reorganising

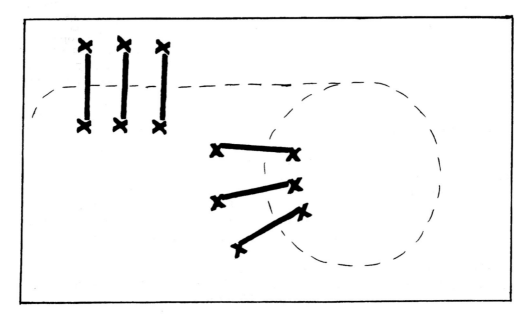

Rising trot. The rider is behind the movement of the horse, the hands are not sufficiently towards the horse's mouth so the horse cannot use his neck properly. The photo clearly shows that the nose is behind the vertical.

is to be avoided, then from the outset they can be erected so that three are placed on the open centre line and three on the straight beside the track on the long side. In the long run every rider will choose his own layouts, so that I shall only make a few suggestions.

Phase 2: Work on circles

The *second phase* is reserved for the actual work on circles. The exercise must not last too long and requires a considerable amount of tact on the part of the rider. At the working trot, sitting, the horse is ridden on the circle. Just in front of the cavalletti the rider will put his hands forward and will be careful to ride exactly in the centre of the ground rails. If the horse responds to the rider's aids,

the next time round the circle will be changed so that the same exercise is ridden on the other rein. If ground rails have been erected on only one circle, then the movement 'change on the figure of eight' will be carried out, by this means a change of rein takes place. Of course the stiff side will be worked most often but experience has taught that a change of rein now and then also helps the stiff side, even if it is only because it takes the horse's attention away from the difficult side and makes him once more happy and willing.

After about 5–10 minutes there must be a short pause, during which the horse will be ridden straight forwards. By riding forwards on the long side of the school there is an opportunity to renew general activity of the horse's action. It is always a good idea to ride forwards if one wants to overcome any stiffness or disobedience. Gustav Steinbrecht's sentence:

'Ride your horse forwards and keep him straight'

Rising trot on a circle on the left rein. The experienced horse has the correct bend and is paying careful attention.

Wrong. The horse drifts to the outside and the inside rein is loose.

should always be uppermost in the rider's mind.

On returning to the circle, to begin with, the centre of the cavalletti will again be ridden. Gradually the rider will try to *enlarge his circle*. Since the distances on the outside are greater the horse must extend himself more. The inside hind foot will be stimulated to the maximum vigour of the tread and at the same time it is required to accept more weight. Now we have almost reached the point between muscle-building training and a conditional break-down caused by over-work. Therefore *on no account* should the enlargement of the circle be ridden more than once or twice on both reins.

Phase 3: Ending on a good note

The *third phase* is to make sure that the lesson finishes happily. The horse should return to his stable in a quiet, contented state of mind so that next day he is willing to begin work. For this reason I recommend that a few simple exercises should be ridden at the end of the lesson. These exercises should be such that one knows that the horse can easily master them.

To finish on a good note is half way towards success next day.

Therefore it is worthwhile as a conclusion to the work on circles to trot a few times straight over the ground rails and after doing this to give the horse a free rein.

Riding over varied lines of cavalletti is a good exercise to improve the rider's feel and to create a better balanced seat as well as providing interest and pleasure. Riders will want to try out every toler-ably sensible suggestion and once it is mastered, then young people look for additional ways of riding. But the riding instructor is reminded that only those exercises that are practical for training purposes should be included. Everything is practical that increases the *pleasure of riding*, improves the seat and does not bring either the horse or the rider into unnecessary danger.

The horse shows good bend but the rider's body stays behind the movement.

Gymnastic Jumping

Gymnastic Jumping

Introduction

In the second part of the book we now deal with the gymnastic jumping part of cavalletti work. This is an integral part of the training of both young horses and novice riders. The use of gymnastic jumping offers an opportunity to improve the weaknesses of horse and rider. The basis for this claim is my extensive experience gained when training dressage, showjumping and eventing horses and riders. I have always been able to call on my father's experiences and I have also had the help over many years of Fritz Ligges' training experiences; these really deserve a book on their own. When in the U.S.A. and Canada I had the opportunity to observe the training methods of Ian Miller. To extend my education I have, amongst others, taken part in Anne Kursinski courses which have had a strong influence on my riding.

The first part of this chapter is mainly about schooling the rider to establish a basis for riding successfully over jumps. The second part of the chapter deals with the inexperienced horse having his first jump and later being introduced to gymnastic jumping. There will also be tips on how to make use of the gymnastic exercises over jumps.

The segregation of horse and rider may seem strange to the reader but I choose to do it this way to explain the various aspects of the training more clearly. In practice horse and rider form one unit and learn together and from each other.

To finish, there are some examples of training plans, though these are only rough guides as they have to be individually worked out according to the horse's and rider's needs.

Gymnastic jumping should be introduced to the rider as an integral part of training. I am especially concerned about specialising too early which is detrimental to both horse and rider. Gymnastic jumping is the most important factor next to dressage for the schooling of showjumpers and riders over showjumping courses. Jumping exercises also have great value for the event horse and rider. In the special discipline of dressage, the mental effect of gymnastic jumping is often undervalued.

Basics

Gymnastic jumping is the exercising of horses over cavalletti, low poles, small obstacles and rows of obstacles. This should give horse and rider the confidence to face show jumps in the ring. Gymnastic jumping teaches the horse to use his body effectively and to think for himself.

The horse should be able to do the exercises with as little interference from the rider as possible; the rider should only support when necessary.

The height of the jumps need not be more than 2–3 ft 3 in (60–100 cm) which is quite sufficient and saves the horse's legs.

Small jumps – big effect!

The building of the gymnastic jumping course should be carefully thought out. Varying the jumps and the distances stops the rider and horse from getting bored.

Be careful not to use just one way of putting up the jumps but choose a way that suits each individual horse.

Trouble can be avoided by building the fences to suit the individual horse so that there are no problems. But if problems do evolve they should be solved not with strictness but with praise to establish a valuable basis of confidence.

Goals (aims)

By using exercises over poles, cavalletti and various obstacles, the different abilities of horse and rider will be developed and improved. They should be developed together not separately. To show quickly what can be achieved with the exercises, the following goals will be briefly explained.

The horse must be active over the first row of jumps so that the rider can fully concentrate on his seat. By following the horse's movements he can improve his balance. The rider has the opportunity to establish and control his seat, which is the basis of his influence on the horse. Furthermore, concentration and co-ordination are needed when the jumps follow each other in quick succession so horse and rider have to react quickly too.

Through establishing a good rhythm the rider will get the feeling of the canter strides which will later help him to establish the speed of the canter. The feel for distances can be achieved by careful riding. The main aim is for rider and horse to have full confidence in each other; both must trust each other's abilities. The exercises have to be built up in such a way that both horse and rider feel comfortable and finish on a happy note. They should both enjoy the work and not feel overstretched.

The most important aim of gymnastic jumping is the strengthening and loosening of the horse's back muscles. Inviting jumps that suit the horse's stride are beneficial to stimulating his back muscles.

The horse has to learn to think for himself and pay attention, this will help him to cope with any problems. It is therefore important to change the jumps around. Take the horse's experience into account: the novice needs more ground lines (see photo on page 108) to secure a safe take-off. These aids can be slowly reduced and eventually taken away.

To improve the horse's reactions, the distances between the jumps should be changed as follows. Short distances teach the horse to shorten his stride and canter in balance. Long distances between jumps make the horse lengthen his stride. Jumping in-and-out jumps (bounces) needs strength and helps to develop strong hindquarters.

In the beginning, the young horse will have problems keeping his balance and finding the right approach to the jump. By changing distances the horse will learn much more quickly as he has to pay more attention to keep his balance than he would when jumping over just single obstacles.

The development of speed and height only applies later to experienced horses.

The construction of an hour's training

Each lesson has to be carefully thought out and systematically built up. The rider or trainer should have a clear idea of what he wants and work on it step by step. If, for example, the aim is to shorten the horse's stride over a row of jumps, he should then, at the end of the lesson, jump over single jumps so that he retains his centre of balance, does not take off too soon and shows a willingness to jump off his hocks.

How often gymnastic jumping is included in the training programme depends entirely on the individual horse and rider. A rough guideline would be working over cavalletti and/or jumps two to three times a week. Young horses especially could benefit from short exercises interspersed with dressage work about four times a week. In any case, one should not overtax horse or rider with too prolonged training. To balance dressage work, jumping once a week is enough.

A rough guide to one hour's training would be:

1. Loosening-up phase
2. Work phase
3. Relaxing phase

These are divided as follows:

1. At least 10 minutes work on a long rein: cavalletti could be included at the walk. About 15–20 minutes easy trot and canter between the jumps. Cavalletti at trot help to relax and loosen-up the horse.

2. Roughly 10–20 minutes jumping, gradually building up the jumps. The rider can decide whether to take walk breaks in between jumping sessions. The ground condition has to be considered as has the horse's reaction to the work. The actual jumping time should not exceed 15 minutes. The rider should stop and let the horse relax before he gets tired.

3. To finish, trot on a long rein and then walk for at least 10 minutes on a loose rein. If possible, a short walk through the woods would be most beneficial for both horse and rider.

A thoughtful and successful hour's work needs time, patience and quiet and should not be carried out in a hurry.

Schooling of the rider

Equipment

The rider should always wear a hard hat (and I don't mean just beginners). A cap with a chin strap is essential when jumping. A cap without a chin strap could easily come off.

As well as a cap, a whip and spurs are an essential part of the equipment. (An inexperienced rider should not wear spurs until he learns to keep his legs still on the horse. Normally every experienced rider should wear short, blunt spurs for use only when the leg aid is ignored. The emphasis is on *blunt* spurs which are quite sufficient to keep the horse listening to the aids.)

It is my opinion that a smack with the whip behind the rider's leg is more effec-

Basic elements for successful riding over jumps

A rider should not start jumping until he is able to ride basic dressage movements and be in control of his horse.

His riding must be so confident that he can give independent aids, e.g. when doing rising trot he must not move his hands up and down.

The horse must accept the rider's aids and respond to, for example, transitions and halts straight away without the help of a long whip and sharp spurs.

If the rider has confidence in his trainer, his own capabilities and his horse, he could start with simple exercises (if he starts with cavalletti as described later on he hardly leaves the ground). When starting to jump he should not be anxious but relaxed. If he is not it is difficult for him to follow the new movements of the horse.

The generous relaxing phase prepared the horse for the coming work.

tive than a continuous tapping with the spurs. The whip should be of medium length, as the horse's mouth can get jabbed when a short whip is used. Too long a whip, on the other hand, hits the hind legs and is not recognised as an adjunct to the rider's leg.

It is necessary for the beginner to have a schoolmaster who is forgiving when mistakes are made. It is not easy to find such a schoolmaster but without one it is hard to establish a good grounding for the rider.

Cap with chin strap.

The key to successful riding is *self-discipline and concentration*. The rider should concentrate on his seat, finding the best way to the jump and he should follow the horse's movements without interfering; he should have no problem if he follows this advice.

Both rider and horse learn through repetition. The important things that the rider has to attend to are the *seat*, *rhythm* and basic gaits. By repeating specified exercises in the correct manner, confidence will be established and the exercises will eventually improve. For instance, counting the canter strides between jumps is helpful for practising a steady canter.

I would like to reiterate that each exercise consists of three phases, a loosening-up period, a jump period and a riding-on period. All phases are equally important in the development of horse and rider.

Jumping over cavalletti needs confidence; an 11-year-old English thoroughbred is used as a schoolmaster.

One often sees a rider spending too much energy preparing for a good jump but losing all concentration after the jump and thereby not being ready for the next one. When jumping a course, the strides after landing are often the approach strides for the next jump.

The most important things to achieve are: fluent and stylish jumping, apart from the seat and balance, (more of this in the next section); looking for the jump in good time; being forward-going and a good canter rhythm. To begin with the rider concentrates on one thing then later, puts everything together so that it comes automatically. This, of course, takes time.

The rider is responsible for three things:
1. taking the best line towards the jump;
2. having the right pace and rhythm;
3. not interfering with the horse at the wrong moment and always keeping the horse on the aids.

The rider must keep the correct pace and the best line to the jump. The jump itself

This 7-year-old Holsteiner gelding has his ears pricked on landing, looking for the next obstacle.

is up to the horse. This is why it looks so easy when top riders are jumping. The rider must change the speed when turning (either shortening or lengthening the stride) to give the horse time to concentrate on the jump. The horse can canter rhythmically and steadily when the pace is established. The canter should be active but contained. The rider should sit lightly to help save his horse's back and not block the movements.

When short canter strides are asked for the horse should be collected and not pulled out of rhythm. When accelerating, the strides should be longer, not rushed and hurried. One often sees a rider losing momentum when turning. This is why I would like to point out:

when turning, keep the momentum, stay balanced and approach the next jump in rhythm.

As soon as the rider has a feeling for the length of his canter strides, he can choose the pace he wants. This helps him to gauge the correct distance for take-off. If the approach to the jump is correct and the horse is on the bit and in balance, there should be no problem finding the right distance for take-off. He can change the canter strides by lengthening or shortening them should the distances be too long or too short. He should only interfere when he realises that the distance is wrong but should not panic because he has the wrong approach to the jump. With continued training the feel for the correct distance will come automatically.

Good long strides in extended canter.

Canter, forward seat

The seat and balance

The rider canters in good balance and looks towards the next jump.

When jumping, the seat raised out of the saddle is also called the 'forward seat', 'light seat' or 'jumping seat'. This can vary from a seat slightly raised out of the saddle to one completely, or nearly so, out of the saddle. Experienced showjumpers have developed their own seat which suits them and the horses they ride.

The jumping seat

- The upper body is inclined forward from the hip.
- During the suspension phase the upper body is forward and the seat out of the saddle so that the rider is in balance.
- He must remain in this position to stay over the horse's centre of gravity.
- The weight of the rider is carried mainly by the thigh, knee and heel.
- The heel of the rider is the lowest point and the stirrup is under the ball of the foot.
- The knee is at a greater angle and pressed hard on the saddle to give the rider the necessary security.
- When taking off there is sufficient pressure on the heel to stop the leg from moving and to remain on the girth.
- Upper arm, elbows and hands are in front of the body.
- Lower arm and reins are in a straight line to the horse's mouth.
- The hands give gently towards the horse's mouth as needed.
- There is a soft contact with the horse's mouth.
- The rider looks straight ahead between the horse's ears.

At this stage I would like to mention the following points. A slightly forward-inclined upper body should swing with the movement. Think of 'kneeling on the saddle'. This makes it easier to get the weight off the saddle, which eases the horse's back. The rider should follow the horse's movements and keep the upper body steady.

Mistake

The upper body is too far forward so the rider 'jumps before the horse' i.e. he is in front of the horse's movement. This makes it difficult for all horses to produce a good jump but it is more difficult for young horses or those who are not well-balanced. If the rider sits too far forward, too much weight is put on the forehand and this makes the jump more difficult.

The rider should sit still until take-off and then go with the horse, but not too early and not incline forward too much. If he misses the moment when he should go with the horse he gets behind the movement and loses balance.

Correction

Jump without stirrups.

The rider should look between the horse's ears, that is, he must be quick to look for the next jump and must also take in the line to the next jump.

Example

When jumping on a curved line the rider should look not only at the first jump but also to where the next jump is so that the complete picture is taken in.
● Look towards the jump early enough.
● When going over a jump look towards the next one.

Horse and rider are in balance.

The heel is the lowest point of the rider. The thigh is in constant contact with the horse, neither too far forward nor too far back. The weight of the rider is lightly carried by the knee and heel.

The position of the lower leg influences the balance and position of the upper body, which is why its correct position is so important for the jumping seat. The lower leg stays flat against the girth with the toes slightly turned out. The leg contact must be light. The rider should not continually tap or press too hard because the horse will become dead to the leg and the rider loses the instant reaction from the horse which is so necessary in showjumping.

While jumping the cavalletto the rider is already looking towards the next obstacle.

The hands must 'follow' over the jump and should be forward and low when taking off. Primarily the arms go forward; the upper body merely follows as necessary. The rider must give as much rein as is necessary for the horse to stretch his neck but still keep a good contact. Beginners should stretch their hands or arms in the direction of the mane so that, if necessary, they can hold on to the mane or support themselves on the neck. It is also better if beginners keep the reins loose and lose the contact for a moment rather than hanging on to the reins and jarring the horse's mouth. The experienced horse knows his job and often jumps better with loose reins as I have observed when watching riders working on exercises for the seat.

After the jump, the contact is lightly taken up again (but should not shift back and forth). It is sometimes a good idea for safety reasons to push the hands forward to the mane to give greater security should the horse throw up his head or make an awkward jump.

A good rider is able to do both: go forward to the horse's mane or his mouth, and is flexible with his hands, depending on the horse he is riding.

Guidelines to be put to practical use

1. Exercise: to canter in a straight line over cavalletti.

This exercise gives the rider the opportunity to get the feel of the movement when riding in the jumping position. At the same time he gets the feel of the canter strides by cantering in a constant rhythm.

A low cavalletto is placed in such a way that it can be jumped from both directions on a straight line. A marker is put on the middle of the jump so that the rider gets into the habit of always jumping over the centre.

The rider starts off by riding in walk over the cavalletto paying attention to coming on a straight line to the centre of the jump and continuing straight. Next he does the same in rising trot paying special attention to keeping the trot fluent and not changing tempo.

The trainer should ensure that, right from the start, the pupil gets used to looking at the cavalletto in good time and looking ahead when jumping.

The phase after the jump is as important as the approach (as explained in the section on basic elements for successful schooling over jumps). To keep the rider concentrating, he should halt after the jump in a straight line. This should be a soft transition and the horse should stay straight.

If the trot work is satisfactory, work in canter can be started.

When cantering over the low cavalletto, the horse will only take a lengthened stride over the jump, which

The rider starts in walk over a low cavalletto.

will help the rider to get used to sitting in the jumping position without getting frightened.

The first jumping exercise consists of four phases:
- approach the jump straight;
- ride over the centre of the cavalletto;
- ride straight on after the jump;
- halt on a straight line.

Depending on the horse's temperament this exercise can also be done in walk and trot. Changing the rein makes the exercise more interesting and so can be repeated more often.

Next, the cavalletto will be turned to its highest point and the exercise repeated at the canter. This will give the rider the feeling of jumping. Experienced horses will normally jump as easily over the higher cavalletto as they did over the lower one and keep their rhythm. When the rider is happy with cantering over the cavalletto, he should take a walk break to relax. While he is doing this, the cavalletto is turned back to its lowest point

The centre of the cavalletto is marked with a red sticker to make it easier for the rider to trot over it.

The rider canters over the low cavalletto in jumping position.

and a second one put up roughly 62–65 ft (19–20 m) away.

The normal length of a horse's canter stride is an average of 11 ft (3.5 m). This length is taken into consideration when putting up the cavalletti. Add one stride for take-off and landing. These measurements vary, of course, with the height of the jumps and the speed they are ridden at. When the jump is low, the distances of take-off and landing shorten, so 62–65 ft (19–20 m) between the jumps is perfectly sufficient. This means that five strides are taken. If the horse canters at normal speed over the first cavalletto, he should then take five strides before jumping the second.

To begin with the pupil trots over both cavalletti in rising trot. He should approach and continue in a straight line. When he has done this on both reins he should do the same in canter. It is important that he pays attention to his seat. The rider should move with the horse and, when over the first of the cavalletti, already be looking towards the second. If this exercise is carried out

successfully, by keeping a straight line and good rhythm, the cavalletti can then be turned to their highest point and the exercise repeated.

The rider should alter the exercise when he is able to ride straight lines after the jump and halt; he could ride a circle or change the rein for a change. The horse will then not always expect to halt but will learn to listen to the rider's aids (an important aspect of showjumping).

The rider has now had his first experience of riding over two small obstacles on a straight line in the jumping seat. This exercise is also useful for advanced riders who want to improve their feeling for canter strides. At the same time they can practise the speed which is necessary to jump with four or six strides, in other words, lengthen or shorten the stride.

Once the first exercises have been accomplished, the rider starts counting the strides between the cavalletti. He should get into the habit of counting out loud so that the trainer can hear whether, for instance, he counted the landing stride (which he may do at the beginning).

Very good straight halt.

The schoolmaster uses only a lengthened stride to jump over the higher cavalletto.

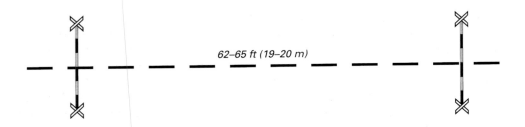

62–65 ft (19–20 m)

Two cavalletti on a straight line.

The rider canters dead straight over both cavalletti.

Counting starts on the first canter stride after landing (1, 2 . . . 5) and a good rhythm must be kept. The speed, suitable for the horse, should be established before turning towards the jump and maintained after the jump until the halt.

The counting of the canter strides is very valuable. It teaches the rider to feel the rhythm and to judge the distances. After a few exercises he knows when he counts '3' he is two strides away from the jump, which helps him to see what the two remaining strides look like. This will help him to develop an 'eye' which tells him whether it is necessary for him to push on or to collect more.

The experienced rider now tries to ride the distances with four canter strides; for this he needs to go faster. He has already learned how to lengthen the stride when he was riding dressage. The only difference here is that he is jumping over two cavalletti. He must already increase speed before turning to face the cavalletti, so that the first cavalletto will be jumped with a lengthened stride. If the rider canters on after the first jump, the four strides will come automatically, thus the rider can keep a light contact with the horse's mouth without losing rhythm on the approach to the second cavalletto.

This exercise can be extended for the experienced rider who could try to put in an additional stride between the jumps by shortening each stride to accommodate six strides.

The preparation begins with shortening the strides. To do this, the rider should sit up more and lower his seat. It is best to have the shortened stride before the first cavalletto so that the six strides occur automatically. If the rider feels after landing that his stride is not short enough, he shortens it still more by, softly, sitting deeper in the saddle and closing the hands. The halt on a straight line concludes the exercise as it has done after previous exercises.

The horse is better balanced and contained when he is working at a collected canter. The centre of gravity is transferred back slightly, so that the rider has to sit up more to keep the proper balance. This exercise can be extended and should be varied by changing the distances. Frequent repetition will soon improve the feeling for the correct approach and speed.

2. Exercise: jumping cavalletti on circles.

An exercise to improve various abilities.

The rider learns to feel at home in the jumping position. He develops the feeling for the rhythm and speed on the circle. The horse will also improve by having to bend on the circle. It is important that the horse does not change legs when jumping cavalletti on the circle or he could fall out of the circle. To avoid this, the rider must ensure that he has a bend to the inside of the circle.

One cavalletto will be put out at its lowest height at the side of the arena on the circle. The first exercise is to jump it on the circle. It is best for beginners to jump on the left side of the cavalletto when on the right rein so that the horse has some support. Always start at the trot to make sure the rider is familiar with the circle and rides it correctly.

In practice it is often not ridden correctly, though the exercise is simple enough. Many riders do not look where they are going early enough and do not follow the line of the circle.

This is ridden on both reins, so that the horse is worked equally. Next, the rider canters over the centre of the cavalletto and then rides round several times on both reins paying attention to the correct seat and rhythm.

If the exercise is completed successfully on both reins, the cavalletto will be moved to the centre of the arena. It is more difficult than it appears to canter on the circle over the cavalletto and carry on cantering on the circle.

To make the exercise more difficult the cavalletto is turned to its highest point to give the rider the feeling of going over a low jump. The experienced horse will continue cantering on with longer strides without rushing or going faster.

The next move is to put up a second cavalletto on the opposite side of the circle. This exercise will first be done in trot over the low cavalletti. Attention must be paid to the most important part of the exercise, that is, the rider has to look well ahead when jumping the first

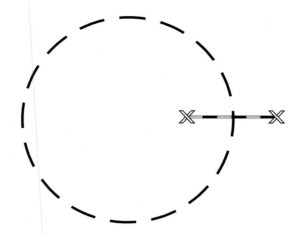

Cavalletto on the circle.

The horse trots in a good position and the correct bend over the cavalletto on the circle.

cavalletto. This will stop him getting into bad habits such as looking down. The rider will thus learn to always look ahead.

Once the rider has mastered this exercise in trot, there should be no difficulty with him doing it in canter. The height of the cavalletti will then be raised and they will be jumped on both reins until the rider can keep a constant rhythm, jump exactly over the centre of the cavalletti and keep the same line without going faster.

The correct execution of these simple exercises is critical. It is important to keep on repeating them to achieve the correct feel and to remember it. For the horse it is only a matter of taking larger canter strides, so he will not be overfaced, although rests are needed now and then.

These basic exercises can be extended for the advanced rider.

One variation is for the rider to ride a figure of eight with a change of rein over one cavalletto, starting off in trot. Two big circles of the same size are ridden. This variation is easier ridden in the indoor school because riders are accustomed to changing the circle there, thus making it easier to keep the shape of the circle.

At the beginning the cavalletto is put at the side of the arena.

Two cavalletti on a circle.

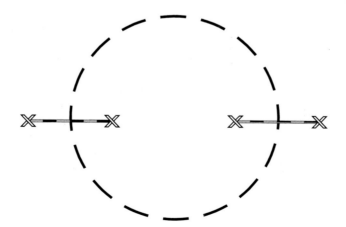

The rider canters on the circle over two cavalletti.

Whenever the rider wants to change direction over the cavalletto he must look in the new direction. The hands also move to show the horse the new direction. Although the rider goes over the cavalletto at an angle, he should still be over the centre.

When the rider is happy with the work in trot, he can start cantering. This should be a working canter. The horse usually changes leg when jumping over the cavalletto and so changes direction.

A second cavalletto could be put on the outside of the circle. The change through the circle can be done either by a simple change (through trot) or a flying change. This exercise helps the rider to make his horse attentive and obedient as he has to really concentrate to jump the cavalletti as well as change the rein.

Over the first cavalletto, the rider looks towards the opposite cavalletto without changing the balance.

Two cavalletti on the outside of two circles ridden on a figure of eight.

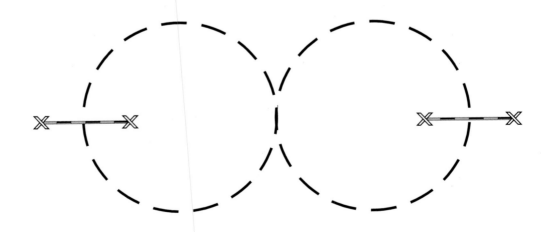

The horse changes legs over the cavalletto.
The rider should stay straight and not drop
his hip.

Change of rein over the cavalletto when
ridden as a figure of eight.

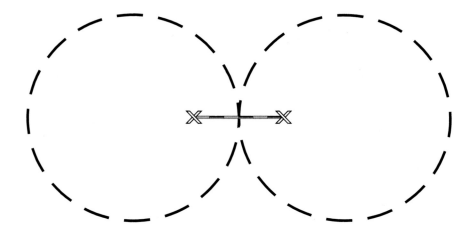

Another variation can be made by placing four cavalletti at equal distances on the circle. One or two helpers are necessary to put up the jumps.

The rider is being taught to always look well ahead to the next jump. This needs quick reactions because the cavalletti follow each other very quickly. Jumping continues on the circle and the cavalletti must always be jumped over the centre. The rider has to keep turning the horse so that he does not fall out of the circle.

Often, the rhythm is not maintained and the horse usually goes faster. After several good rounds, a walk break should be taken. It is important to remember to do the exercise on both reins. The rider should not be bothered about how many canter strides are taken, nor whether the horse has the correct distance on take-off. The horse is responsible for this and will sort himself out, especially when the cavalletti are low.

The exercises will help to educate the horse to jump smoothly and obediently on circles. Instead of cavalletti, low jumps could be used. If so, someone should be at the jump to put it up quickly if necessary.

The rider has had his first experience jumping over cavalletti in the jumping position. A foundation has now been laid for jumping over a line of fences and gymnastic jumping. I have given advice for building simple courses in the section on course variations for inexperienced horses (page 105). The education of the rider can now be advanced step-by-step by referring to these suggestions. The tips for single jumps are also relevant for several jumps.

Four cavalletti equally placed on the circle.

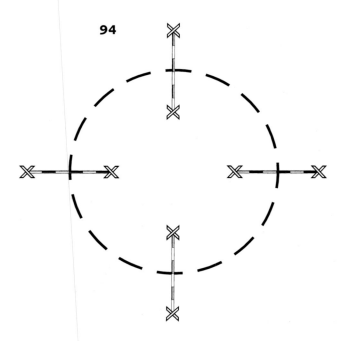

94

Typical mistakes and tips for correction

Cavalletti on the circle.

The following examples are not suitable for the complete beginner who is just establishing his jumping position. While the beginner is mastering his seat, the trainer has to note any weaknesses and correct them. The seat has to be correct before the aids have any influence and only then can the horse be supported and helped.

The horse pays attention when cantering to the next cavalletto.

This section is specially aimed at riders who feel that faults have crept in (perhaps because of a lack of help with the seat). If the mistakes have become established the rider has to concentrate hard to change them and experience tells us that it takes time to correct them. If the rider *is* aware of the mistakes, he has to work hard to get rid of them until doing the correct thing becomes second nature.

Work over cavalletti is especially useful for correcting the seat as quite a lot of cavalletti work can be done without overworking the horse.

When the correct 'jumping seat' has been established over cavalletti, the rider

can go on to jumping lines of fences.

The rider should concentrate completely so that it is not necessary to keep repeating the jumps. Before approaching a jump he should think about the correction he has made to his seat.

Mistake

When jumping, the rider does not look ahead but at the neck of the horse.

Correction

The trainer or helper stands some way in front of the line of jumps and raises a hand and fingers. When jumping the rider looks towards the raised hand and counts the fingers out loud. The rider could also help himself by fixing his eyes on an object ahead of him (a tree, a chair etc.)

Mistake

The rider does not look at the next jump early enough.

Correction

A line of low jumps is put up between four other jumps (see pages 117 and 122). The rider is instructed to look left over the first jump, then right over the second, left over the third and right again over the fourth. A firm, balanced seat and an ability to react quickly are needed for this. The rider should be able to turn his head quickly from side to side so that he can keep the jumps in sight but without losing his balance.

Mistake

The rider rests his hands on the horse's neck during the jump and/or landing.

The rider is looking down and consequently twists his upper body.

The rider looks at the raised hand of the trainer and counts the fingers.

Correction

Jumping without reins with the arms stretched out or the hands on the hips prevents the rider from resting his hands on the horse's neck. This exercise, like the previous one, should be done over a line of low fences. The reins are knotted so that they cannot get in the way. Initially, the rider should only let go of the reins over the last jump, then, gradually, over all the jumps. The rider lets go of the reins as soon as the horse is over the first jump.

The trainer need not worry about the horse; horses often jump better when they are free.

This is also a small test to see how the horse manages without contact with the rider's hands and the reins.

The following exercise is designed to establish the position of the rider's hands.

The rider should consciously move his hands towards the mane, then towards the horse's mouth, holding the reins wide and not touching the neck. This teaches the rider to use his arms and hands independently from his seat to keep his balance.

Mistake

The rider does not sit in balance.

Correction

To jump without stirrups.

Whether riding dressage or jumping, the best way to establish balance is to ride without stirrups. It is easier for the rider to sit in balance without stirrups and so keep his position when jumping. This makes it impossible for him to get 'in front' of the horse which would interfere with the horse's movements.

The inexperienced rider should never try this before he really wants to, or if he is frightened.

The rider can have either both arms outstretched or have his hands on his hips

The more secure a rider feels with the stirrups, and if he has built up his confidence, the sooner he can start.

To begin with, the rider removes the stirrups after a low jump then rides a circle without stirrups. He will be closer to his horse as soon as he takes his feet out of the stirrups; the seat relaxes, his body moves more in harmony with the horse, the leg lengthens and the lower leg lies quietly on the horse's side. When the rider feels safe the stirrups will be removed from the saddle; if left hanging or crossed over the saddle, they could interfere with the horse.

To begin with, one cavalletto is jumped, then two in a straight line, then when used to this, a rider can progress to lines of low jumps. As the jumps follow

each other quickly in a line, it helps the rider to feel the movement of the centre of gravity.

The more a rider is able to keep his balance without the help of reins or stirrups, the more effective and safe he will be. Horses are often more relaxed and contented when riders jump without stirrups because they are more careful and find it easier to go with the movement.

A very well-balanced rider. The horse jumps safely and independently with ears pricked.

The rider is not in balance but is in front of the horse's movement.

During the landing phase the rider's feet are out of the stirrups.

To get used to jumping without stirrups the rider jumps just one cavalletto.

This rider sits in very good balance even without stirrups.

Schooling the horse

Equipment

As well as a saddle, bridle and, perhaps, a martingale, boots are necessary to protect the horse's legs. Various types of brushing boots and perhaps overreach boots are used.

Bitting remains much the same as it does for dressage and depends on the level of the horse's education. The bit should not be too thin or sharp for daily use. Some riders try to overcome difficulties by using stronger bits instead of working harder on the basic dressage. It is much better to have patience and to try to work out the problem. An experienced rider might sometimes use a sharper bit, which has been tested at home, when competing. For specially sensitive horses an ordinary snaffle with a double-jointed mouthpiece can be used.

Depending on the horse's education

The correctly equipped showjumper.

and reliability, a martingale may be used to prevent him from raising his head too high. The martingale should be long enough not to interfere with the rider's hands or the horse's mouth.

In passing

As we have seen in earlier sections, the rider is responsible for the approach and speed. Before he reaches the first element of the jumps (cavalletti or low obstacles) he moves his hands forwards to give the horse the necessary freedom to cope by himself as much as possible without interference. (Education for independence.)

With a young horse, the phase of riding on after the jump should be given special attention so that he learns to listen to the rider and wait for his instructions. To keep the horse's attention, the rider should either change pace, make a circle or change the rein and, to make it more interesting, the jump should be approached from different directions.

Repetition is boring

Gymnastic jumping demands a very high concentration from the horse so rest periods are important. These should not be fixed but dictated by the rider's feelings. It is my opinion that you cannot lay down the regularity and frequency for jumping. One day the horse will learn by repetitive jumping over a line of cavalletti, at another time he will get bored with it. The worst thing that can happen is that the horse will get careless if asked to jump the same fences over and over again. It requires a special feeling and understanding on the part of the rider; the aim is to keep the horse's interest and pleasure in jumping alive.

The following are a few guidelines for bringing on young horses. Be careful not to treat them all the same. Here again, it is most important that riders and trainers understand their horses. The gymnastic jumping work must be different for every horse, taking into consideration their temperament, size of canter stride, natural ability and enjoyment of jumping as well as their stage of education.

Conditions the horse has to fulfil

The horse should understand the rider's aids and respond to them with confidence and in a relaxed manner and carry out transitions and halts correctly. The horse should be prepared for his first jump under a rider by being loose jumped over cavalletti and trotted over coloured poles.

A line of jumps (grid) should be built with the correct distances between them. The jump poles are then taken away before work starts and put on the ground at right angles next to the wings so when required for building the jumps again the wings will dictate the correct distances. A line of three to four poles or cavalletti can be put down for trotting over when starting off, then the jumps can be added progressively.

Varied courses for inexperienced horses

A young horse should learn right from the start to jump any sort of fence and that it is not acceptable to stop or run out. Once he understands this, he will start to enjoy his jumping. This means that, in practice, the rider should have no hesitation in being firm when jumping the first low fences (even in walk, if necessary). If the horse is nervous it is good to encourage him with the voice or have a lead horse. Once the horse has learned to jump the fence with confidence, he can

A completed grid of gymnastic jumps.

The same grid from the front with the blue oxer and red upright poles laid next to the stands ready for use. A white pole lies on the ground in front of the yellow cross poles, the other white pole will be pulled in later.

progress to jumping over a number of obstacles.

It is useful to have wings on the jumps to help inexperienced horses. The first jumps should be built facing the exit and on the side of the school wall; the wall guides and helps the horse.

When building a variety of jumps, let the horse get used to the new sights and surroundings by letting him have a good look at the jumps.

That is why I start the lesson with the work phase, assuming that the horse has been walked to loosen him up prior to working. Two poles are necessary for an upright jump, one being put 1 ft (30 cm) in front of the jump to make the take-off easier.

At the beginning, each oxer needs three poles: two oxer poles and one on the ground underneath the front oxer pole. The oxer poles can either be of equal height or the back pole can be up to two holes higher.

Inviting fences should be used when the horse first starts jumping. No poles should be on the ground (apart from

This grid is jumped at walk and then slowly built up.

A lead horse jumps in front.

A natural boundary on one side of the jump and wings on the other are helpful for inexperienced horses.

To help the novice with a safe take-off, a ground line is necessary.

The lower pole of the oxer lies directly under the top pole, not in front of it.

ground lines). The jumps should be wide-faced, at least 11 ft (3.5 m).

Poles will sometimes be put on the ground between the jumps. Because poles can slip it might be better to use cavalletti at their lowest height or a board (although this makes course building difficult) but I have never known a horse hurt himself by slipping on a pole. It is useful to have some spare poles handy; they might be needed for extra wings.

When going over the first jump it is important for the rider to have a soft contact with the horse's mouth. If he should lose the contact too early, the horse will feel abandoned. At the beginning it is advisable to move the hands forward in the direction of the mane. Should the horse misbehave or throw his head up, the rider can grab the mane or support himself on the neck. The rider must not take too tight a hold over the jump because the horse must be able to

develop confidence, to stretch his neck and balance himself with a rounded back and long neck.

With cavalletti spaced for trot work, the rider aims the horse at the centre of the cavalletti. When the horse has trotted quietly over the low cavalletti on both reins, he can be put over the highest level of the cavalletti with a distance of 7 ft (2.2 m) between them. (This distance will depend on the size of the horse and the length of his trot stride.) Cross poles can also be used.

The wings and boundary should prevent the horse from escaping sideways. Should the horse hesitate, he should be made to go over the poles in walk or from a standstill.

The horse should be rewarded and made a fuss of so that he feels confident right from the start.

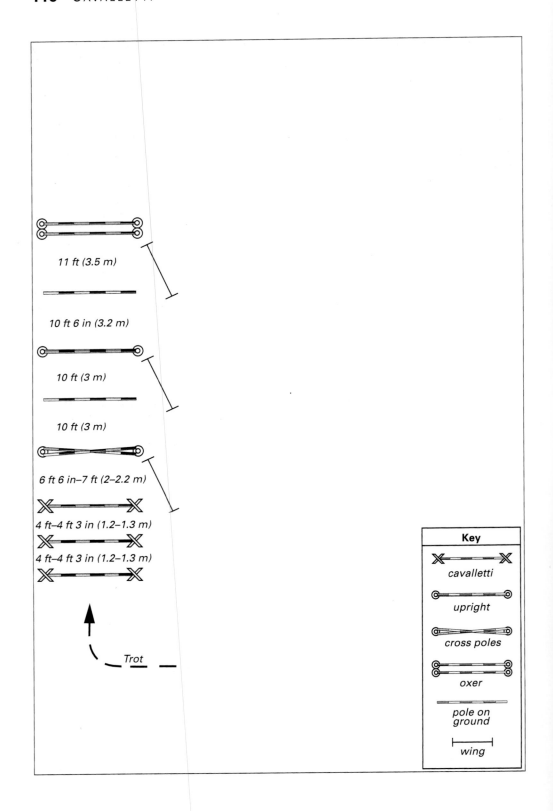

11 ft (3.5 m)

10 ft 6 in (3.2 m)

10 ft (3 m)

10 ft (3 m)

6 ft 6 in–7 ft (2–2.2 m)

4 ft–4 ft 3 in (1.2–1.3 m)

4 ft–4 ft 3 in (1.2–1.3 m)

Trot

Key

cavalletti

upright

cross poles

oxer

pole on
ground

wing

First grid for novice horses.

A soothing voice and a pat on the neck relaxes the horse and relieves any anxiety he may have. There are horses that concentrate so hard on trotting over cavalletti that they try to trot over the higher jumps. If this happens, it is a good idea to put up cross poles, which make the horse want to jump over the centre of the jump.

The next step is to put a pole on the ground at 20–21 ft (6–6.5 m) away so that the horse will canter over it after jumping the cavalletti. Finally, a small upright should be built and jumped a few times. There is no hard and fast rule as to how often the gymnastic jumping line should be jumped.

If, for example, an oxer with a bottom rail is built, followed by an upright and then another oxer, then, after jumping these two or three times, the distances can be shortened ready for the next step.

If a horse rushes any of the jumps they should be approached at an angle so that the horse cannot hurry on the approach.

Should the horse slow down or hesitate, canter along the long side of the school and collect him in the turn to gain some impulsion. It is often advisable to reduce the cavalletti to one instead of three to keep the momentum going.

Start again two or three days later by putting a pole on the ground 10 ft (3 m) behind the highest-level cavalletti or cross poles, then the upright. Bit by bit the build up of the course will continue. Following the upright, a pole is placed on the ground at 10 ft 6 in (3.2 m), after 11 ft (3.5 m) another pole is placed on the ground then an upright followed by an oxer.

The 4-year-old Trakehner gelding bravely follows the experienced horse over his first row of jumps.

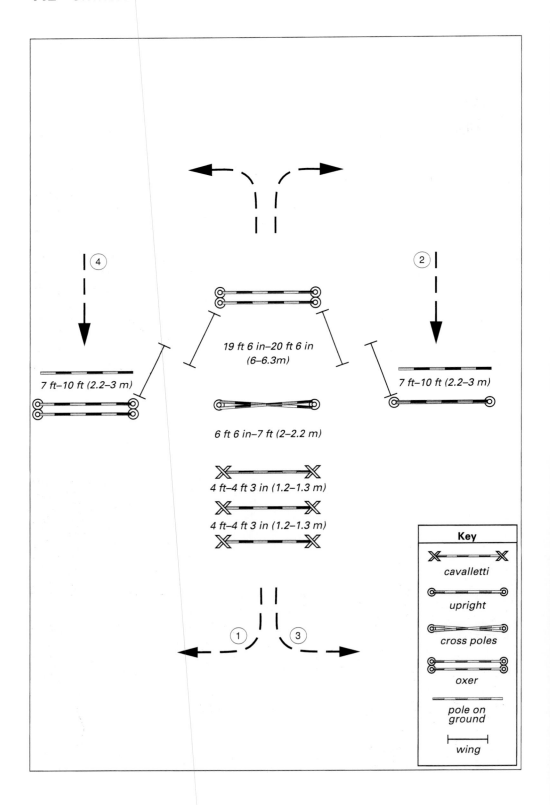

19 ft 6 in–20 ft 6 in
(6–6.3m)

7 ft–10 ft (2.2–3 m)

7 ft–10 ft (2.2–3 m)

6 ft 6 in–7 ft (2–2.2 m)

4 ft–4 ft 3 in (1.2–1.3 m)

4 ft–4 ft 3 in (1.2–1.3 m)

Key

cavalletti

upright

cross poles

oxer

pole on ground

wing

An open-sided grid on the centre line.

If these jumps are put up in stages the horse will gain confidence over each one. Should he hesitate or refuse, a lead horse should be used a few times and then he should be jumped on his own again. To finish, an upright should be built on the opposite side, with a pole 7 ft (2.2 m) in front. At the end of the line of jumps, the horse should be brought back to trot, jumped over the upright out of trot, asked for a half-halt and then jumped down the grid again. This process could be repeated a few times.

When a second jump is added, it is advisable to put a pole under the first jump. The horse is often so interested in the second jump that he forgets about the first one and makes a mistake.

The advantage of building up the fences in the middle of the school (see diagram on page 112) is that they can be approached on both reins and there is no need to stop. This will be the first time that the horse jumps without the support of the boundary. To begin with, wings should be used and then taken away later on.

This exercise should be started with three to four cavalletti spaced for trot and special attention must be paid to them being jumped over the centre. Later, the cross poles will be added at a distance of 7 ft (2.2 m). The jumps shown on the long side of the school should not have been put up at this point so that the rider can use the whole school. The leg the horse lands on determines whether he is turned left or right at the end of the grid and he is then asked for a half-halt in the corner. After a while the rider will be able to do this on the straight line after landing.

A pole in front of the jump helps an inexperienced 4-year-old to work out the distance for take-off.

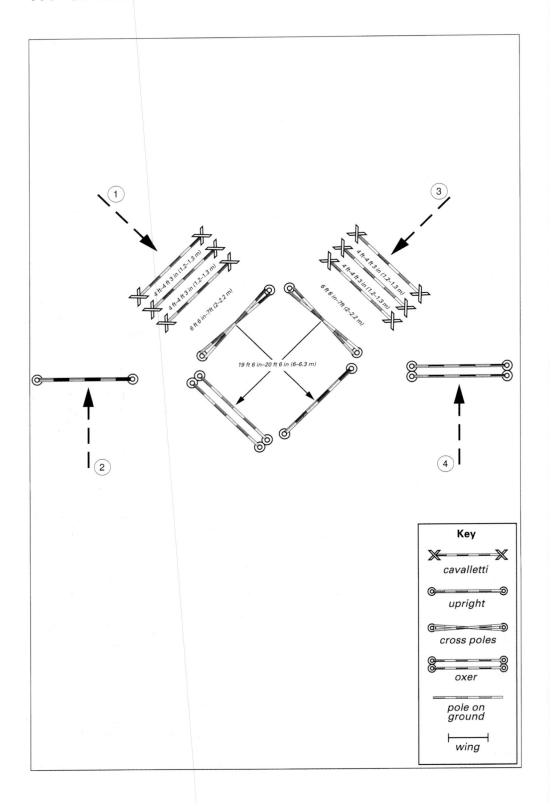

Key

cavalletti

upright

cross poles

oxer

pole on ground

wing

A grid on the diagonal.

The next step is to put a pole on the ground followed by an upright and finally an oxer. The gymnastic grid should be solidly built as it will be jumped more frequently in connection with the single jumps to give the horse his necessary confidence.

After the grid, the rider turns, trots over the pole on the ground 7 ft (2.2 m) in front of the upright jump and jumps the upright. Next time he turns the other way, trots over the pole 7 ft (2.2 m) away from the oxer, then jumps the oxer; to begin with the two elements of the oxer should be close together. Finally the individual exercises are put together: the rider trots on the left rein over the jumps in the centre, canters on the right rein and jumps over the pole which is 10 ft (3 m) from the upright; before the corner he trots, turns towards the centre and jumps the grid again, finally he keeps cantering on the left rein and jumps the pole and oxer.

If the horse completes the course successfully he must be given a deserved break.

The course on page 114 is designed to keep the horse straight on the diagonal.

The course should be so well prepared that the stands are in position and the poles lie next to them ready for use. The 3–4 cavalletti at trotting distance apart are on the diagonal so that they can be used for the relaxing phase.

To start with, the cross poles are jumped after the cavalletti at a distance of 7 ft (2.2 m). The rider trots through the first diagonal, asks for a half halt, trots the diagonal length of the school then turns and jumps the second diagonal grid, then trots the diagonal length of the school again. Next, an upright jump will be put in at about 19 ft 6 in–20 ft 6 in (6–6.3 m) on one diagonal followed by an oxer on the other diagonal.

It is now time for the horse to have a break and be walked on a long rein. This time could be used by the assistants to put up an upright and an oxer opposite each other on the long sides. Depending on how the horse feels and how he managed the grid exercises, the rider must decide whether or not he should put a low cavalletto or a pole at 10 ft (3 m) to help with the take-off over the single jumps and, perhaps, to put wings on them.

If a horse tires easily the number of cavalletti can be reduced to one and that one will help with the take-off. Running out at the second jump will be prevented because it is framed on both sides.

To finish, we will put the various exercises and jumps together, as follows. The rider trots on the left rein towards the diagonal and trots over the cavalletti and cross poles, starts canter and jumps over the upright. He then canters on a straight line and jumps over the centre of the upright on the long side, goes back to trot, turns towards the diagonal, trots over the cavalletti and cross poles, goes into canter and jumps the oxer. The horse should carry on cantering and jump the oxer on the long side. If this exercise is successful, give the horse a break. The rider should make sure that the horse jumps in good rhythm and stays straight before and after the jumps. If the horse speeds up too much in the canter, ride a circle.

The sequence of jumps can be changed as required to ensure that the horse approaches them with confidence. The variety of jumps can now be extended and can either be built on the track or in the middle of the school. The advantage of building them on the track is that the side of the

A novice 4-year-old Trakehner mare trots over the cavalletti, jumps over the cross poles, canters on and jumps over the oxer.

school forms a boundary and the rest of the school can be utilised. If the grid is built up in the middle of the school, the advantage is that it can be approached on both reins and the course can be continued on either rein. It should be possible to jump the single jumps on both reins (four poles are necessary if the oxer is to be jumped from both directions).

After the horse is loosened up, the grid will be built up, i.e. the grid can be completed. Something should be added to the line when the horse has jumped it successfully so that he keeps on being faced with a new situation.

The distance between the jumps will vary according to the horse's stride so that he can jump easily within his capa-bility. He should be able to concentrate on the four successive jumps without having to alter his stride. Consequently, the distances given are only a rough guide.

Should the horse stop or try to run out, turn him and bring him into the jump once more. If he jumps, then the whole grid should be jumped again. There are horses who find it difficult to suddenly jump several jumps in a row and it does not make sense to keep on trying. It is better to take a break, let the horse relax, then try again over an easier grid until eventually he jumps the whole grid.

If the horse is getting too strong, place a pole between each jump to calm him down.

A grid of poles for gymnastic jumping is also suitable for teaching the jumping seat.

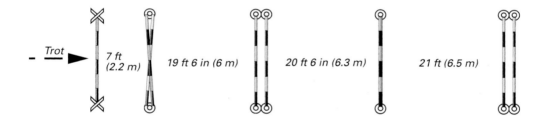

Trot

7 ft (2.2 m)

19 ft 6 in (6 m)

20 ft 6 in (6.3 m)

21 ft (6.5 m)

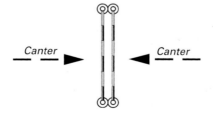

Canter

Canter

By varying the jumps you will keep even an experienced horse interested.

A pole on the ground between the jumps teaches the horse to develop a rhythmic canter.

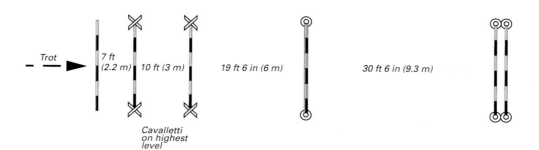

Trot
7 ft (2.2 m) | 10 ft (3 m) | 19 ft 6 in (6 m) | 30 ft 6 in (9.3 m)

Cavalletti on highest level

Beginning in-and-out work with a grid.

In-and-Outs

In-and-outs are small obstacles without room for a canter stride between them; as soon as the horse lands, he has to take off again. Once the horse is able to move with a swinging back and his head down, the in-and-outs can be incorporated into the training. Although this work improves the action of the horse's back, you must be careful not to overdo it. It might be asking too much of the horse if the obstacles are too high or repeated too often.

Start the horse off with either two high cavalletti or cross poles. To make the take-off easier put a low cavalletto or a pole 7 ft (2.2 m) in front of the first jump and one behind it at 10 ft–11 ft (3–3.3 m). This distance can be extended when the horse has learned the principles. The in-and-outs can, with thought, be

The in-and-out grid must be built up slowly in order not to overface the horse.

The in-and-out grid consists of five obstacles and three poles on the ground.

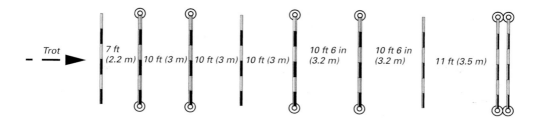

Trot
7 ft (2.2 m) | 10 ft (3 m) | 10 ft (3 m) | 10 ft (3 m) | 10 ft 6 in (3.2 m) | 10 ft 6 in (3.2 m) | 11 ft (3.5 m)

A complete row of in-and-out jumps; the horse is jumping with concentration.

The horse is not jumping over the centre of the jumps. The photo on the right shows how a horse can be taught to jump over the centre by jumping cross poles.

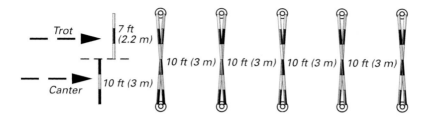

Trot ▶ 7 ft (2.2 m)

10 ft (3 m) | 10 ft (3 m) | 10 ft (3 m) | 10 ft (3 m)

Canter ▶ 10 ft (3 m)

In-and-out grid of cross poles.

included in the gymnastic training.

The in-and-out grid demands great concentration and dexterity of the horse, so each obstacle should be low and more or less of the same height. More elements will be added gradually once he has jumped the first ones successfully.

The rider should turn into the first element in trot and the approach should be short and straight. If the rider approaches straight from too far out the horse can be disorientated by the number of jumps. A variation of the in-and-out can be achieved by putting up a line of cross poles which have the advantage of teaching the horse to jump in the centre.

Start with one pole on the ground and a cross pole jump 7 ft (2.2 m) distant, then slowly build up the cross pole jumps one by one. Another possibility is to lie all the poles on the ground in their correct position then, one by one, make them into cross poles. To change the rein, a cavalletto is put 7 ft (2.2 m) in front of the last cross poles so that the grid can be approached from the other side.

The demands can be increased by placing a pole 10 ft (3 m) in front of a jump and approaching it at canter. The distances will now be shorter, so the horse has to jump in greater balance and be more active. The rider must decide whether three cross poles are enough for a young horse or if he can cope with five. I would not recommend using more than

Either start off with one pole and one cross pole jump . . .

. . . or put several cross poles on the ground and put them up one by one.

five in-and-outs at a time as there could be a danger of asking too much of the horse.

There are infinite possibilities for gymnastic jumping grids. It depends on how the rider aims to build the courses, which sort of in-and-outs are used, how many canter strides and the result the instructor is looking for.

Grids are also useful for improving the rider's seat and for solving or preventing any difficulties the horse may have (see the following section on Typical Mistakes and Tips for Correction).

Some gymnastic jumping can, of course, be ridden at a canter but only if the horse and rider are secure in trot. See the following examples.

I do not want to go too deeply into schooling techniques but simply to show the way to a solid basis for further education.

Typical mistakes and tips for correction

Mistake

The horse gets too strong after the last jump and bucks or runs off.

Correction

On landing, take up a light contact and halt with use of the voice. If the horse bucks, keep his head up and, for safety, lean backwards a little. The horse should be turned and ridden in a circle. The frequently used method of riding towards a wall and halting should, in my opinion, only be used as a last resort because it unsettles the horse.

Do not be too hard or rough with the hands when halting. If the horse gets frightened of hard hands because his

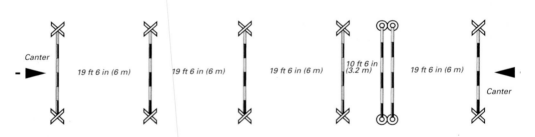

This grid can be approached from both sides in canter.

Cavalletti grid to improve rhythm (above).

A grid that needs concentration and attention (below).

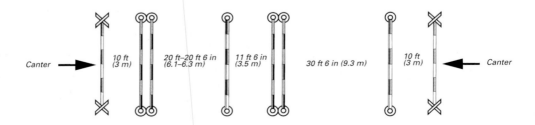

*A steady canter over cavalletti before an oxer
with horse and rider in good rhythm.*

*A good jump over an oxer out of canter: Ingrid
Klimke on a six-year-old gelding.*

mouth has been hurt, he will stiffen up over the jump.

The following exercise will help to control the horse after the jump. The rider trots over a cavalletto facing the wall and stays on the figure of eight until the horse is settled. An alternative is having an assistant who stands with outstretched arms some way behind the jump so that the rider has to check in front of her and halt.

Mistake

The horse is rushing in front of the jumps.

Correction

Approach the first element at an angle. The following three to four cavalletti are all placed on a curve so that the horse has to concentrate hard to keep his footing. The rider goes towards the grid a few times without jumping; he must keep the horse's attention. If an assistant stands in

front of the first jump, the halt will be much easier for the horse. (If an assistant is used in this way, both rider and assistant must pay the utmost attention to safety.)

Mistake

The horse speeds up too much through the grid.

Correction

An assistant walks up and down, preferably between the last two jumps, so that the horse looks down at her and forgets to rush. (Again, rider and assistant must pay attention to safety.)

Two cavalletti placed against one another against the wall.

Short side of school.

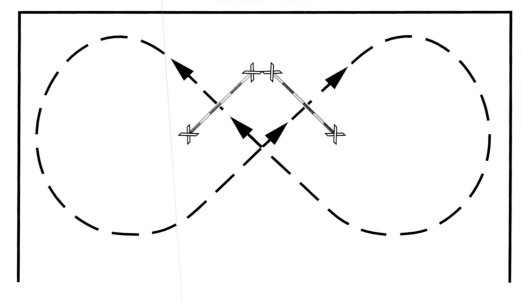

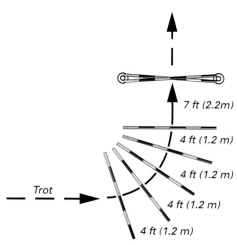

7 ft (2.2m)

4 ft (1.2 m)

4 ft (1.2 m)

Trot

4 ft (1.2 m)

4 ft (1.2 m)

Trotting poles on the turn before the grid.

from his mistakes and will be more careful and attentive in future.

Mistake

The horse always jumps to one side, in this example the left.

Correction

The rider puts his left hand on the mane with the whip in the left hand and turns the horse to the right with the right hand. He stands the horse in front of the jump, uses the whip once, turns right once and continues coming out of the turn. You must be consistent about this.

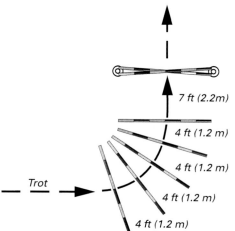

Poles put at an angle within the grid to improve the horse's concentration.

Mistake

The horse jumps flat, is careless and inattentive.

Correction

The poles should be put at an angle, with the poles lower on one side than the other. The horse has to concentrate in order not to make mistakes. The assistant could also walk up and down behind the last fence. Where experienced horses are concerned, the ground poles could be removed. The rider should not worry if the horse makes a mistake. The horse has to learn

Mistake

The horse is uncertain in his approach and goes from side to side.

Two poles on the ground make a lane to 'lead' the horse into the jump.

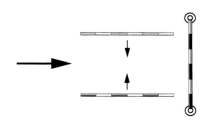

Correction

Make a lane by placing two poles on either side and in front of the jump. In order not to upset the horse, the poles should be placed wide apart. Once the horse is used to them, the lane can be narrowed so that the horse has to jump over the middle of the jump.

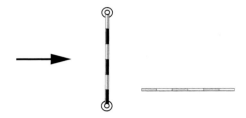

A pole behind the jump stops the horse from jumping crooked.

Mistake

The horse jumps crooked and lands to one side of the jump.

Correction

A pole is put on the ground behind the jump at a right angle to the jump. To avoid the horse landing on it, it should be placed quite a distance from the jump. Ideally, he should make his first canter stride after landing parallel to the pole.

To begin with, the poles are placed the full width of the jump apart. They can then be moved inwards and then removed later on.

The horse cannot get away to the left.

Example

The horse keeps drifting to the left and lands to the left. In this case, the pole has to be placed to the left of centre 6 ft 6 in–10 ft (2–3 m) from the jump. Be careful! To begin with it should lie at the edge of the jump and only gradually be rolled in towards the middle. The horse has to land straight to achieve a good jump. Mistakes will soon appear if he twists over the jump. The poles can either be put at the side of the grid or the crookedness is corrected over a single jump. Either way, there are poles on either side and in front and behind the jump. The middle of the upright is approached at a canter and the rider keeps the horse in canter after the jump, turns him and jumps it from the other direction, also in a straight line.

Another solution is to make a lane with poles on either side of the jump which will teach the horse to approach straight, jump straight and keep straight after the jump.

Two poles help to teach the horse to jump straight.

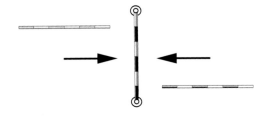

Definite ground lines and two poles at 10 ft (3 m) distance.

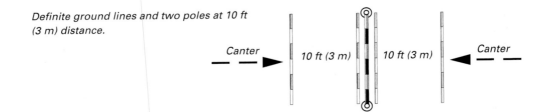

Canter →   10 ft (3 m)   10 ft (3 m)   ← Canter

Mistake

The horse finds it difficult to work out the correct take-off point.

Correction

A ground pole is placed in front of the upright. It must be at least the width of the jump. The horse finds it easier to concentrate on the ground line and achieves a better bascule over the jump.

A further aid is to put a pole 10 ft–10 ft 6 in (3–3.2 m) in front of the

A safe jump and great leap over the pole behind the jump.

jump. Even if the horse is not correct when approaching the pole, he will be correct for the jump. If a pole is put behind the jump at 10 ft (3 m) the horse will pay more attention to landing and not rush off. This exercise can be carried out easily on both reins at canter.

The examples I have given should illustrate all the possible variations of exercises and help the rider find the right combination for the individual needs of horse and rider. Careful thought should be given to the aim and usefulness of the exercises and they should then be carried out without rushing. It is also most important to remember to praise the horse.

I hope that my suggestions and tips will have shown many riders and trainers the advantages of gymnastic jumping as a valuable alternative to the usual daily routine, especially for the horses.

Appendix:
Plans for Training

Appendix: Plans for Training

The plans for training are based on the premise that they are simply a basis for cohesive schooling. They do not pretend to be a ready-made directive, since they are only based upon a part of the education of horse and rider – work with cavalletti and jumping – other work being mentioned simply in passing. Individual characteristics are always the decisive factor as to what may be achieved in every single case.

However there are some basic rules that must be considered by all who are interested in the success of this method of training. The following plans are chiefly built upon these rules and give the rider a criterion for a systematic programme.

I assume that the majority of riders will differentiate between summer and winter schooling. During the summer many riders are at shows or are taking part in other forms of sport, whilst actual training is likely to be done more during the winter months. It is for this period that these plans have been made. They encompass a period of from four to six weeks.

In addition to the individual riding lessons there are certain principles to which the rider must pay attention. Every schooling period is divided into three parts: suppling-up, relaxing and the actual schooling exercises that are to be carried out. Suppling-up which is done before cavalletti work usually lasts from 10–15 minutes. The exact legnth of time depends upon the horse's willingness, conformation, age, temperament and how much he has been ridden. Relaxing at the walk with a free rein serves to quieten him and to ensure that he returns to his stable in a happy frame of mind. Generally about 10 minutes are needed.

The middle part of the schooling period is given up to work over the cavalletti.

Four to Six Week Plan for Basic Schooling (for horses in their second year of schooling)

A horse's basic schooling must be sufficiently comprehensive to allow for all the branches of equestrianism. For this reason it covers all tests which are expected of a riding horse at horse shows etc. One must take care not to specialize too soon, and one should remember that the road to the top leads simply and surely over the widest possible basic schooling.

FIRST WEEK:

Keynote: To get used to working with ground rails at the walk and trot.

Monday: No training. The horse should not stay in the stable all day long but be led out for at least 30 minutes. If possible, the following would be of benefit for the horse: hacking out, or being turned loose in the school or outdoor paddock.

Tuesday:
1 Begin with cavalletti work without the rider. Duration of work about half an hour consisting of:

(a) free work	or *(b)* on the lunge
Phase 1 & 2	Phase 1 & 2
(see pp. 24–25)	(see pp. 29–30)
15 minutes	15 minutes
Phase 3	Phase 3
(see pp. 25–26)	(see pp. 30–32)
15 minutes	15 minutes

2 In addition about 10 minutes riding over cavalletti at the walk (see p. 39).
3 Conclude with a little dressage, then ride on a free rein to relax.

Wednesday:
1 About 15 minutes suppling up at the walk, trot and canter on both reins.
2 Then about 20 minutes cavalletti work under the rider, on straight lines, beginning with the walk and one rail (see p. 39), then at the trot (see pp. 46–59); in between 5 minutes rest.
3 Some dressage exercises and a few minutes on a free rein to relax.

Thursday: no cavalletti work; depending on the weather, either a quiet hack round the countryside or an hour's dressage, tiring the horse as little as possible.

Friday:
1 5–10 minutes to supple up.
2 A half-hour of ridden cavalletti work on straight lines, beginning with the walk, with increase in distances for the medium walk (see pp. 40–43), then at the trot, towards the end over increased distances (see p. 56); in between 5 minutes rest.
3 A few dressage exercises at the canter and then ride on a free rein until the horse is relaxed and ready to return to his stable.

Saturday: as Thursday.

Sunday: According to the weather, either: ride outside with jumping over small, natural obstacles, uphill work, quiet cantering on even ground.
or:
In the riding school: suppling up; some dressage exercises to improve submis-

sion; then canter in the forward seat on both reins; concluding with one or two jumps from the trot and canter.

SECOND WEEK:

Keynote: Consolidation of the first week's lessons.

Monday: No training.

Tuesday:
1 A good 15 minutes to supple up, during which occasionally a free rein over the cavalletti on straight lines.
2 About 20 minutes at the walk and trot over cavalletti on straight lines; as far as possible, beginning with several cavalletti.
3 A few dressage exercises at the canter and ride on a free rein to relax before returning to the stable.

Wednesday: As for Thursday of the first week.

Thursday:
1 About 15 minutes to supple up.
2 A short half hour of ridden cavalletti work on straight lines at the walk and trot with strides between (see pp. 40 & 59) and with increased distances (see p. 56); between each exercise a short 5 minute pause.
3 Some dressage and walk to relax.

Friday: As for Thursday of the previous week.

Saturday: either
1 Free jumping or cavalletti work without the rider, going free or on the longe.
2 Dressage.
3 Walk to relax.

or:

as for Thursday of the second week.

Sunday: As for Sunday the first week or as for Thursday of the second week.

THIRD WEEK:

Keynote: Habituation to work over ground rails at the canter and gymnastic jumping.

Monday: No training.

Tuesday: As for Tuesday of the second week.

Wednesday:
1 About 15 minutes to supple up.
2 About 15 minutes cavalletti work at the trot on straight lines.
3 About 10 minutes cantering in the forward seat on both reins, including a few times over ground rails (see pp. 62–63).
4 Walk to relax.

Thursday: As for Thursday of the first week.

Friday:
1 About 15 minutes to supple up.
2 Some dressage exercises to improve submission.
3 Gymnastic jumping with one cavalletto and one obstacle.
4 Walk to relax.

Saturday: As for Thursday of the first week.

Sunday:
1 About 15 minutes to supple up, including a few times at the walk on a free rein over cavalletti on straight lines.
2 About 10 minutes cantering at the forward seat on both reins.

3 Gymnastic jumping with continual changes of building.
4 Walk to relax.

FOURTH WEEK:

Keynote: Consolidation of the third week's lessons.

Monday: No training.

Tuesday: No cavalletti work; dressage exercises with plenty of suppling up work.

Wednesday: As for Wednesday or Friday of the third week.

Thursday: As for Tuesday.

Friday:
1 About 15 minutes to supple up, including occasional walk on a free rein over cavalletti on straight lines.
2 About 10 minutes cantering in the forward seat on both reins.
3 Gymnastic jumping with several cavalletti in front of the obstacle (see p. 123).
4 Walk to relax before returning to the stable.

Saturday: Depending on the weather, go out hacking, or dressage.

Sunday:
1 15 minutes to supple up.
2 Either basic training over cavalletti, poles, single jumps or showjumping course.
3 Walk to relax.

FIFTH WEEK: No cavalletti work; increased dressage work and whenever possible hack out.

SIXTH WEEK: Repeat the most important exercises of the first four weeks without demanding too much of the horse.

After the sixth week it should be possible for the horse to have complete confidence in all the basic cavalletti exercises on straight lines, including some gymnastic jumping. From the seventh week on, with alternations, extra emphasis will be placed on those exercises that have a definite bearing on the desired schooling target. Now work on circles and half-circles can be used to further this.

It should not be difficult to continue to work independently, in view of the experience gained during the first six weeks. Problems will constantly occur during the course of schooling. In most cases they be solved by returning to easy exercises and then again slowly increasing the difficulty to the stage required.

Four to Six Week Plan for a Dressage Horse

This plan is based on the understanding that the basic schooling has been successfully completed. Once again it is limited simply to work over cavalletti as part of the entire system of training. Whatever other demands may be made are dependent upon the stage of schooling which the dressage horse has reached. To that extent everything is valid that is written in any good instruction book on dressage, on the gradual building up of dressage exercises.

FIRST WEEK:

Monday: No training.

Tuesday:
1 About 20 minutes suppling exercises on both reins in all three gaits, concluding with trot and walk over cavalletti on straight lines.
2 Exercises to improve submission, at the same time practising correct transitions and walking on a long rein over the ground rails, to renew the cadence of the walk.
3 Ride straight forward, chiefly at the trot.
4 Walk to relax before returning to stable.

Wednesday: No cavalletti work.

Thursday: Cavalletti work at the trot, concluding with increased distances to improve activity and the scope of the movement (see pp. 46–57).

Friday: No cavalletti work.

Saturday: Preferably no cavalletti work, except at the walk on a free rein during the period of suppling up, or free cavalletti work (see pp. 24–28), or free jumping.

Sunday: Ride prescribed exercises.

SECOND WEEK:

Monday: No training.

Tuesday: No cavalletti work.

Wednesday: Cavalletti work at the walk over shortened distances to improve the collected walk (see pp. 43–44).

Thursday: No cavalletti work.

Friday: No cavalletti work except, to supple up, a little exercise rising to the trot over cavalletti on straight lines.

Saturday: Cavalletti work at the trot, concluding with sitting trot over shortened distances to improve the expression of the movement (see p. 50–51).

Sunday: Ride prescribed exercises.

THIRD WEEK:

Monday: No training.

Tuesday: Cavalletti work free (see pp. 24–28).

Wednesday: No cavalletti work.

Thursday: No cavalletti work, except at the walk on a free rein during suppling up.

Friday: As for Thursday of the first week.

Saturday: No cavalletti work.

Sunday: Ride prescribed exercises.

FOURTH WEEK:

Monday: No training.

Tuesday: As for Tuesday of the first week.

Wednesday: No cavalletti work.

Thursday: Cavalletti work at the walk, concluding with increased distances to improve the scope of the movement (see p. 43).

Friday: No cavalletti work.

Saturday: As for Saturday of the second week.

Sunday: Ride prescribed exercises.

FIFTH WEEK: No cavalletti work; instead dressage and relax by going for a ride in the country (depending on the weather).

SIXTH WEEK: Repeat the most important exercises of the first three weeks, as well as a few lessons from the plan for basic schooling.

Cavalletti work on circles may also be included as required. Apart from this, deviations can be made when the goal of the schooling on a particular day has not been reached, so that the following day has to be given to repetition. In order to avoid the danger of overtiring the horse it is important to stick to the plan and to limit cavalletti work to only two or three days in the week.

Four to Six Week Plan for a Showjumper

Again it must be understood that basic schooling has been successfully completed.

FIRST WEEK:

Monday: No training.

Tuesday:
1 A longish period of suppling up with cavalletti work at the trot on straight line, rising trot.
2 Canter forward seat.
3 Some exercises to improve submission.
4 Quiet walking to relax.

Wednesday:
1 Supple up.
2 Exercises to increase willingness.
3 Gymnastic jumping concluding with one or two single jumps.
4 Walk to relax.

Thursday: Dressage or (according to weather) quiet hack in the country.

Friday: Dressage and jump a few easy obstacles from canter.

Saturday: (Depending on the weather) cross-country with uphill work and easy canter on even ground or dressage.

Sunday: Jumps on straight lines and circles.

SECOND WEEK:

Monday: No training.

Tuesday:
1 Loosen up

2 Some exercises to improve the horse's way of going.
3 Canter over cavalletti or low jumps in jumping position.
4 Ride on loose rein to cool off.

Wednesday: Either free work over cavalletti followed by dressage for loosening up; cavalletti work in trot on curved lines; canter work to improve gait; ride on loose rein to cool off.

Thursday: Gymnastic jumping.

Friday: Dressage.

Saturday: Showjumping.

Sunday: No training.

THIRD WEEK:

Monday: As for Tuesday of the first week.

Tuesday: Gymnastic jumping, asking for more effort.

Wednesday: As for Tuesday of the second week.

Thursday: As for Thursday of the first week.

Friday: Suppling up; cavalletti work at the canter and jumping over combinations.

Saturday:
1 Supple up.
2 Canter to improve condition on both reins, pausing in between to walk.

3 Walk to relax, and to quieten horse; a few times at the walk over the cavalletti with a free rein, on straight lines.

Sunday: Showjumping using colourful and strange jumps for the course.

FOURTH WEEK:

Monday: No training.

Tuesday: Either:
(depending on the weather) long period suppling up outside, concluding with dressage.
or:
as for Tuesday of the first or second week.

Wednesday: As for Wednesday of the first week.

Thursday: Dressage.

Friday: Riding varied distances over cavalletti on curved lines.

Saturday: Like Thursday of the first week.

Sunday: Showjump in unfamiliar place.

FIFTH WEEK:

Increase dressage; perhaps some loose jumping, cavalletti work, competition-level jumping in unfamiliar surroundings.

SIXTH WEEK:

Repetition of the most important exercises of the first three weeks; jumping doubles and treble combinations.

Suggestions for Building Cavalletti for Young Riders

The most important thing in equestrian instruction for children and young people, is to encourage pleasure and confidence in their relationship with horses. A relaxed seat that goes with the movement is the best basis for later achievements. One avoids drawing special attention to learning the dressage seat. The upright position of the upper part of the body for this seat is so often completely misunderstood in the early stages of learning to ride. And it can, therefore, lead to stiffness, to the exaggerated so-called 'military' seat, which does not produce sufficient elegance.

Correct development can be achieved by riding over ground rails. It is essential, through the most varied building of these, to encourage the rider's concentration to the accomplishment of the required exercises, so that constraint and rigidness are automatically forgotten.

It is for this purpose that the four designs for building cavalletti shown in this section have been made. They are simply to encourage riders and to show what can be done with simple resources. Each of these designs allows for a great number of new figures through circles, about turns, and serpentines, so that finally no difficulties should appear if one wants to achieve variations in the lesson or programme. Of course, it is up to individuals to think up other ways of building cavalletti.

Suggestions for building cavalletti for young riders

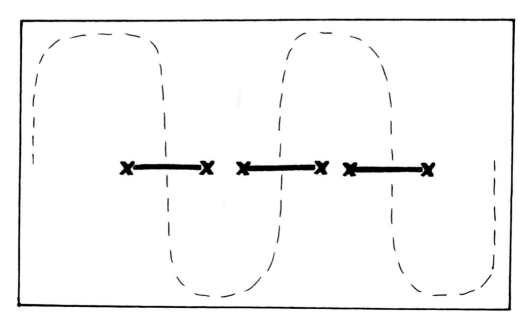

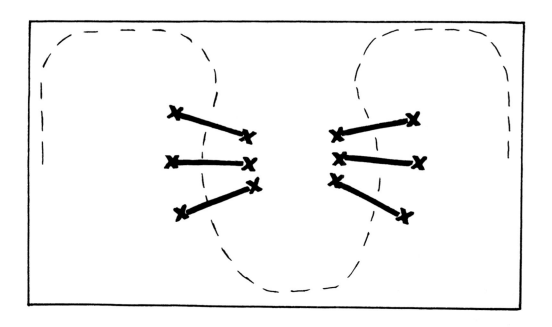

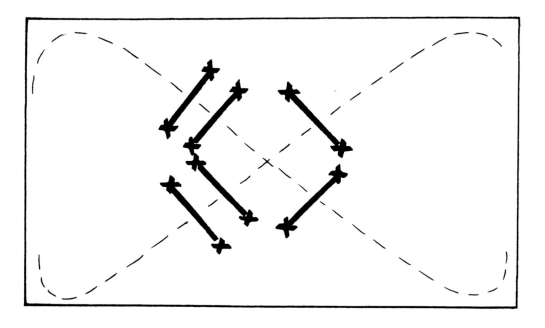

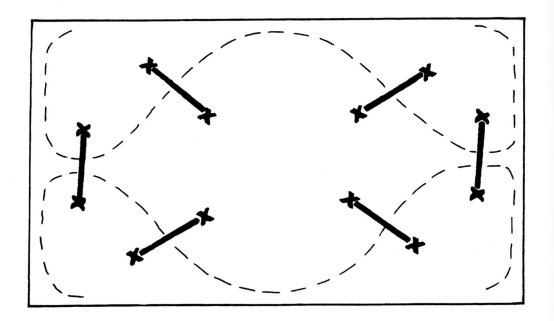

Index